Mindfulness of Breathing
(Ānāpānasati)

About the Author

Bhikkhu Ñāṇamoli (Osbert Moore) was born in England in 1905 and graduated from Exeter College, Oxford. In 1948 he came to Sri Lanka, where he was ordained the following year at the Island Hermitage near Dodanduwa. He spent almost his entire monk's life of eleven years in the quietude of the Hermitage. In 1960, on one of his rare outings, he suddenly passed away due to heart failure. During his life in the Sangha Ven. Ñāṇamoli translated into lucid English some of the most difficult texts of Theravāda Buddhism. His *The Life of the Buddha* and *The Path of Purification* (*Visuddhimagga*) are also published by the BPS.

Mindfulness of Breathing
(Ānāpānasati)

Buddhist Texts from the Pāli Canon
and
Extracts from the Pāli Commentaries

Translated from the Pāli by

Bhikkhu Ñāṇamoli

Buddhist Publication Society
Kandy • Sri Lanka

Buddhist Publication Society
P.O. Box 61
54, Sangharaja Mawatha
Kandy, Sri Lanka

First published 1952
Sixth edition 1998

ISBN 955–24–0167–4

Typeset at the BPS

Printed in Sri Lanka by
Karunaratne & Sons Ltd.
647, Kularatne Mawatha
Colombo 10

CONTENTS

Principal References
and Abbreviations

Translator's Foreword
to the First Edition

Ānāpānasati, or "mindfulness of breathing," is among the Buddhist methods of mind training given most prominence in the Pāli Canon.

It was originally for his own use that the translator collected the material that follows from the Pāli Canon and its commentaries. The idea was to have "under one cover," for the purpose of study, the Pāli teaching on this meditation subject, omitting nothing important and eliminating repetitions.

In the Vinaya and Sutta Piṭakas, the description, or as it might be termed, the "statement," of *ānāpānasati* appears as a fixed formula; it is repeated unchanged in many different settings. Instructions for the "practice" are detailed in the Venerable Buddhaghosa's work, the *Visuddhimagga*. The canonical *Paṭisambhidāmagga,* a technical work dealing with the analysis of different kinds of knowledge, devotes a self-contained treatise to it, which could be called the "Theoretical Analysis." These works have their commentaries, too.

The 118th discourse of the Majjhima Nikāya has been chosen as possibly the most comprehensive single discourse on the subject. In the compressed rendering of the *Paṭisambhidā Ānāpānakathā* an attempt has been made to short-cut the forbidding maze of repetitions and yet preserve intact its strongly formalistic pattern.

Translations have been done afresh where previous ones exist. This was for the sake of consistency. If has been an aim—but only an aim—to render consistently, as far as possible, the same Pāli words by the same English equivalents where the same meanings are referred to throughout these texts. This is in order that the same concepts should be recognizable in different contexts throughout the English, as in the Pāli.

Also, English words carrying specially inappropriate overtones have been avoided as much as possible. Pāli is, above all, a precise language; and it has unique linguistic distinction, too, since it has never been employed outside the field of Theravāda Buddhism. So its words have no alien echoes. But it follows that no translation can reproduce the limpidness of the original.

It would be a mistake to think that every detail given here must be learnt before any progress in meditation can be made. Rather it is the outline (as given in the sutta and the Venerable Buddhaghosa's description of the practice) that should be followed: the details are there for the purpose of settling problems, if they arise.

Ānāpānasati is one branch of the mental training known as the "four foundations of mindfulness" (*cattāro satipaṭṭhānā*) and called "the only path for the realizing of Nibbāna." They are described in the 22nd discourse of the Dīgha Nikāya and the 10th discourse of the Majjhima Nikāya. The same two discourses—the former in greater detail—connect up the foundations of mindfulness with the privotal doctrine of the Four Noble Truths (*cattāri ariya-saccāni*), on which all aspects of the Teaching converge.

"It is through not discovering, bhikkhus, not penetrating the Four Noble Truths that both I and you have been traversing the round of rebirths for so long. Which four? It is through not discovering, not penetrating the noble truth of suffering, the noble truth of the origin of suffering, the noble truth of the cessation of suffering, the noble truth of the the way leading to the cessation of suffering" (DN II 90).

Ānāpānasati is one of the methods for penetrating the Four Truths. The concluding words of the Majjhima Nikāya are these:

"There are, Ānanda, these roots of trees, these empty places. Meditate, Ānanda, do not delay, lest you regret it later. This is our instruction to you."

Ñāṇamoli

Island Hermitage
Dodanduwa
8 October 1952

Preface to the Second Edition

This anthology was first issued in 1952, in cyclostyled form. The production of it had been undertaken as a personal labour of love and devotion by Mr. D.V.P. Weerasinghe of Bandarawela (Ceylon). Since the limited number of copies produced was soon exhausted, there were, throughout the years, repeated requests for a reprint of this work. A new edition was finally undertaken at the request of Mrs. Irene R. Quittner of London, who defrayed the costs of printing that edition.

In parts of the present edition, wherever it appeared preferable, some of the earlier terminology and phrasings have been replaced by those chosen in the Venerable Author's later works, i.e., for Part I, in his translation of the Majjhima Nikāya (in manuscript), and for Part II, in his translation of the *Visuddhimagga*.

The Venerable Author, a bhikkhu of English descent, passed away on 8th March 1960, aged 55—a deep-felt loss to the Sangha and to Pāli scholarship.

The Editor

August, 1964

Namo tassa Bhagavato Arahato
Sammā Sambuddhassa

Part I

THE DISCOURSE ON RESPIRATION-MINDFULNESS
(Ānāpānasati Sutta—MN No. 118)

Introduction

Thus have I heard. At one time the Blessed One was living at Sāvatthī, in the palace of Migāra's mother, in the Eastern Park, together with many very well-known elder disciples—the Venerable Sāriputta, the Venerable Mahā-Moggallāna, the Venerable Mahā-Kassapa, the Venerable Mahā-Kaccāyana, the Venerable Mahā-Koṭṭhita, the Venerable Mahā-Kappina, the Venerable Mahā-Cunda, the Venerable Anuruddha, the Venerable Revata, the Venerable Ānanda, and other very well-known elder disciples. Now at that time the elder bhikkhus were teaching and instructing the new bhikkhus: some elder bhikkhus were teaching and instructing ten new bhikkhus; some elder bhikkhus were teaching and instructing twenty new bhikkhus; some elder bhikkhus were teaching and instructing thirty new bhikkhus; some elder bhikkhus were teaching and instructing forty new bhikkhus. And these new bhikkhus, taught and instructed by the elder bhikkhus, successively achieved high distinction.[1]

And at that time, on the Assembly Day (*uposatha*) of the fifteenth, on the night of the Pavāraṇā ceremony,[2] when the moon was full, the Blessed One was seated in the open surrounded by the Order of bhikkhus. Then, surveying the silent Order of bhikkhus, he addressed the bhikkhus thus:

"I am content, bhikkhus, with this progress; I am content at heart, bhikkhus, with this progress. Therefore, strive still more strenuously to attain the unattained, to achieve the unachieved, to realize the unrealized.[3] I shall wait here at Sāvatthī for the Komudi (moon) of the fourth month."[4]

The bhikkhus of the countryside heard: "The Blessed One, it seems, will wait there at Savatthī for the Komudi (moon) of the fourth month." And those bhikkhus of the countryside left for Sāvatthī to see the Blessed One. And the elder bhikkhus were still more strenuously teaching and instructing the new bhikkhus: some elder bhikkhus were teaching and instructing ten new bhikkhus; some elder bhikkhus were teaching and instructing twenty new bhikkhus; some elder bhikkhus were teaching and instructing thirty new bhikkhus; some elder bhikkhus were teaching and instructing forty new bhikkhus. And those new bhikkhus, taught and instructed by the elder bhikkhus, successively achieved high distinction.

Now, at that time, on the Assembly Day of the fifteenth, on the night of the Komudi moon of the fourth month when the moon was full, the Blessed One was seated in the open surrounded by the Order of bhikkhus. Then, surveying the silent Order of bhikkhus, he addressed the bhikkhus thus:

"Free from chatter, bhikkhus, is this community, free from idle talk, bhikkhus, is this community; it is purified and consists purely of heartwood.[5] Such, bhikkhus, is this Order of bhikkhus; such, bhikkhus, is this community.

"Such a community, bhikkhus, as is worthy of gifts, worthy of hospitality, worthy of offerings, worthy of homage, as is an incomparable field of merit for the world—such, bhikkhus, is this Order of bhikkhus; such, bhikkhus, is this community.

"Such a community, bhikkhus, that a small gift given to it becomes great, and a great gift greater—such, bhikkhus, is this Order of bhikkhus; such, bhikkhus, is this community.

"Such a community, bhikkhus, as it would be hard for the world to see its like—such, bhikkhus, is this Order of bhikkhus; such, bhikkhus, is this community.

"Such a community, bhikkhus, as would be worth travelling many leagues with a knapsack to see—such, bhikkhus, is this Order of bhikkhus; such, bhikkhus, is this community.

"There are, bhikkhus, in this Order of bhikkhus, bhikkhus who are arahats, in whom the cankers are destroyed, who have lived the life, done what is to be done, laid down the burden, reached the highest good, destroyed the fetters of being, and, through knowing rightly, are liberated—such bhikkhus, indeed, are there, bhikkhus, in this Order of bhikkhus.

"There are, bhikkhus, in this Order of bhikkhus, bhikkhus who, with the destruction of five lower fetters,[6] will reappear spontaneously (in the Pure Abodes) and there attain complete extinction without ever returning here from that world—such bhikkhus, indeed, are there, bhikkhus, in this Order of bhikkhus.

"There are, bhikkhus, in this Order of bhikkhus, bhikkhus who, with the destruction of three fetters,[7] and the attenuation of greed, hate, and delusion, are once-returners; returning once to this world, they will make an end of suffering—such bhikkhus, indeed, are there, bhikkhus, in this Order of bhikkhus.

"There are, bhikkhus, in this Order of bhikkhus, bhikkhus who, with the destruction of three fetters, are stream-enterers, and being no more subject to states of woe (and) assured (of their future), are headed for full enlightenment—such bhikkhus, indeed, are there, bhikkhus, in this Order of bhikkhus.

"There are, bhikkhus, in this Order of bhikkhus, bhikkhus who dwell devoted to the practice of the four foundations of mindfulness[8]—such bhikkhus, indeed, are there, bhikkhus, in this Order of bhikkhus.

"There are, bhikkhus, in this Order of bhikkhus, bhikkhus who dwell devoted to the practice of the four right efforts[9]—such bhikkhus, indeed, are there, bhikkhus, in this Order of bhikkhus.

"There are, bhikkhus, in this Order of bhikkhus, bhikkhus who dwell devoted to the practice of the four roads to power[10]—such bhikkhus, indeed, are there, bhikkhus, in this Order of bhikkhus.

"There are, bhikkhus, in this Order of bhikkhus, bhikkhus who dwell devoted to the practice of the five faculties[11]—such bhikkhus, indeed, are there, bhikkhus, in this Order of bhikkhus.

"There are, bhikkhus, in this Order of bhikkhus, bhikkhus who dwell devoted to the practice of the five powers[12]—such bhikkhus, indeed, are there, bhikkhus, in this Order of bhikkhus.

"There are, bhikkhus, in this Order of bhikkhus, bhikkhus who dwell devoted to the practice of the seven factors of enlightenment[13]—such bhikkhus, indeed, are there, bhikkhus, in this Order of bhikkhus.

"There are, bhikkhus, in this Order of bhikkhus, bhikkhus who dwell devoted to the practice of the noble eightfold path[14]—such bhikkhus, indeed, are there, bhikkhus, in this Order of bhikkhus.

"There are, bhikkhus, in this Order of bhikkhus, bhikkhus who dwell devoted to the practice of amity—such bhikkhus, indeed, are there, bhikkhus, in this Order of bhikkhus.

"There are, bhikkhus, in this Order of bhikkhus, bhikkhus who dwell devoted to the practice of compassion—such bhikkhus, indeed, are there, bhikkhus, in this Order of bhikkhus.

"There are, bhikkhus, in this Order of bhikkhus, bhikkhus who dwell devoted to the practice of altruistic joy—such bhikkhus, indeed, are there, bhikkhus, in this Order of bhikkhus.

"There are, bhikkhus, in this Order of bhikkhus, bhikkhus who dwell devoted to the practice of equanimity[15]—such bhikkhus, indeed, are there, bhikkhus, in this Order of bhikkhus.

"There are, bhikkhus, in this Order of bhikkhus, bhikkhus who dwell devoted to the practice of meditation on the foul[16]—such bhikkhus, indeed, are there, bhikkhus, in this Order of bhikkhus.

"There are, bhikkhus, in this Order of bhikkhus, bhikkhus who dwell devoted to the practice of perception of impermanence[17]—such bhikkhus, indeed, are there, bhikkhus, in this Order of bhikkhus.

"There are, bhikkhus, in this Order of bhikkhus, bhikkhus who dwell devoted to the practice of respiration-mindfulness.

Respiration-mindfulness

"Respiration-mindfulness, bhikkhus, developed and repeatedly practised, is of great fruit, of great benefit; respiration-mindfulness, bhikkhus, developed and repeatedly practised, perfects the four foundations of mindfulness; the four foundations of mindfulness, developed and repeatedly practised, perfect the seven enlightenment factors; the seven enlightenment factors, developed and repeatedly practised, perfect clear vision and deliverance.

"And how developed, bhikkhus, how repeatedly practised, is respiration-mindfulness of great fruit, of great benefit?

The Method: The Four Tetrads

"Here, bhikkhus, a bhikkhu, gone to the forest, or to the root of a tree, or to an empty place, sits down; having folded his legs crosswise, set his body erect, established mindfulness in front of him, ever mindful he breathes in, mindful he breathes out.

FIRST TETRAD (Contemplation of the body)

(i) "Breathing in long, he knows, 'I breathe in long'; or breathing out long, he knows, 'I breathe out long.'

(ii) "Breathing in short, he knows, 'I breathe in short'; or breathing out short, he knows, 'I breathe out short.'

(iii) "'Experiencing the whole body (of breath), I shall breathe in,' thus he trains himself; 'experiencing the whole body, I shall breathe out,' thus he trains himself.

(iv) "'Calming the bodily formation, I shall breathe in,' thus he trains himself; 'calming the bodily formation,' I shall breathe out, thus he trains himself.[18]

SECOND TETRAD (Contemplation of feeling)

(v) "'Experiencing rapture, I shall breathe in,' thus he trains himself; 'experiencing rapture, I shall breathe out,' thus he trains himself.[19]

(vi) "'Experiencing bliss, I shall breathe in,' thus he trains himself; 'experiencing bliss, I shall breathe out,' thus he trains himself.

(vii) "'Experiencing the mental formation, I shall breathe in,' thus he trains himself; 'experiencing the mental formation, I shall breathe out,' thus he trains himself.

(viii) "'Calming the mental formation, I shall breathe in,' thus he trains himself; 'calming the mental formation, I shall breathe out,' thus he trains himself.

THIRD TETRAD (Contemplation of mind)

(ix) "'Experiencing the mind, I shall breathe in,' thus he trains himself; 'experiencing the mind, I shall breathe out,' thus he trains himself.

(x) "'Gladdening the mind, I shall breathe in,' thus he trains himself; 'gladdening the mind, I shall breathe out,' thus he trains himself.

(xi) "'Concentrating the mind, I shall breathe in,' thus he trains himself; 'concentrating the mind, I shall breathe out,' thus he trains himself.

(xii) "'Liberating the mind, I shall breathe in,' thus he trains himself; 'liberating the mind, I shall breathe out,' thus he trains himself.

FOURTH TETRAD (Contemplation of mental objects)

(xiii) "'Contemplating impermanence, I shall breathe in,' thus he trains himself; 'contemplating impermanence, I shall breathe out,' thus he trains himself.

(xiv) "'Contemplating fading away, I shall breathe in,' thus he trains himself; 'contemplating fading away, I shall breathe out,' thus he trains himself.[20]

(xv) "'Contemplating cessation, I shall breathe in,' thus he trains himself; 'contemplating cessation, I shall breathe out,' thus he trains himself.

(xvi) "'Contemplating relinquishment, I shall breathe in,' thus he trains himself; 'contemplating relinquishment, I shall breathe out,' thus he trains himself.[21]

"That is how respiration-mindfulness, developed and repeatedly practised, is of great fruit, of great benefit.

Perfection of the Four Foundations of Mindfulness

"And how developed, bhikkhus, how repeatedly practised, does respiration-mindfulness perfect the four foundations of mindfulness?

A. (i–iv) "On whatever occasion, bhikkhus, a bhikkhu, breathing in long, knows, 'I breathe in long'; or breathing out long, knows, 'I breathe out long'; breathing in short, knows, 'I breathe in short'; or breathing out short, knows, 'I breathe out short'; trains thus: 'I shall breathe in experiencing the whole (breath) body'; trains thus, 'I shall breathe out experiencing the whole (breath) body'; trains thus, 'I shall breathe in calming the bodily-formation;' trains thus, 'I shall breathe out calming the bodily formations'—on that occasion, bhikkhus, a bhikkhu abides contemplating the body in the body, ardent, clearly comprehending, mindful, having put away covetousness and grief regarding the world.[22]

"I say that this, bhikkhus, is a certain body among the bodies, namely, respiration. That is why on that occasion, bhikkhus, a bhikkhu abides contemplating the body in the body, clearly comprehending, mindful, having put away covetousness and grief regarding the world.

B. (v–viii) "On whatever occasion, bhikkhus, a bhikkhu trains thus, 'I shall breathe in experiencing rapture'; trains thus, 'I shall breathe out experiencing rapture'; trains thus, 'I shall breathe in experiencing bliss'; trains thus, 'I shall breathe out experiencing bliss'; trains thus, 'I shall breathe in experiencing the mental formation'; trains thus, 'I shall breathe out experiencing the mental formation'; trains thus, 'I shall breathe in calming the mental formation'; trains thus, 'I shall breathe out calming the mental formation'—on that occasion, bhikkhus, a bhikkhu abides contemplating the feelings in the feelings, ardent, clearly comprehending, mindful, having put away covetousness and grief regarding the world.

"I say that this, bhikkhus, is a certain feeling (experience) among feelings (experiencings), namely, the giving attention completely to in-breathing and out-breathing. That is why on that occasion, bhikkhus, a bhikkhu abides contemplating the feelings in the feelings, ardent, clearly comprehending, mindful, having put away covetousness and grief regarding the world.

C. (ix–xii) "On whatever occasion, bhikkhus, a bhikkhu trains thus, 'I shall breathe in experiencing the mind'; trains thus, 'I shall breathe out experiencing the mind'; trains thus, 'I shall breathe in gladdening the mind'; trains thus, 'I shall breathe out gladdening the mind'; trains thus, 'I shall breathe in concentrating the mind'; trains thus, 'I shall breathe out concentrating the mind'; trains thus, 'I shall breathe in liberating the mind'; trains thus, 'I shall breathe out liberating the mind'—on that occasion, bhikkhus, a bhikkhu abides contemplating the mind in the mind, ardent, clearly comprehending, mindful, having put away covetousness and grief regarding the world.

"I do not say, bhikkhus, that there is development of respiration-mindfulness in one who is forgetful and does not clearly comprehend. That is why on that occasion, bhikkhus, a bhikkhu abides contemplating the mind in the mind, ardent, clearly comprehending, mindful, having put away covetousness and grief regarding the world.

D. (xiii–xvi) "On whatever occasion, bhikkhus, a bhikkhu trains thus, 'I shall breathe in contemplating impermanence'; trains thus,

'I shall breathe out contemplating impermanence'; trains thus, 'I shall breathe in contemplating fading away'; trains thus, 'I shall breathe out contemplating fading away'; trains thus, 'I shall breathe in contemplating cessation'; trains thus, 'I shall breathe out contemplating cessation'; trains thus, 'I shall breathe in contemplating relinquishment'; trains thus, 'I shall breathe out contemplating relinquishment'—on that occasion, bhikkhus, a bhikkhu abides contemplating mental objects in mental objects, ardent, clearly comprehending, mindful, having put away covetousness and grief regarding the world.

"Having seen with understanding what is the abandoning of covetousness and grief, he becomes one who looks on with complete equanimity. That is why on that occasion, bhikkhus, a bhikkhu abides contemplating mental objects in mental objects, ardent, clearly comprehending, mindful, having put away covetousness and grief regarding the world.

"That is how respiration-mindfulness, developed and repeatedly practised, perfects the four foundations of mindfulness.

Perfection of the Seven Enlightenment Factors

"And how developed, bhikkhus, how repeatedy practised, do the four foundations of mindfulness perfect the seven enlightenment factors?

A. (1) "On whatever occasion, bhikkhus, a bhikkhu abides contemplating the body in the body, ardent, clearly comprehending, mindful, having put away covetousness and grief regarding the world —on that occasion, unremitting mindfulness is established in him.

"On whatever occasion, bhikkhus, unremitting mindfulness is established in a bhikkhu—on that occasion the mindfulness enlightenment factor is aroused in him, and he develops it, and by development it comes to perfection in him.

"Abiding thus mindful, he investigates, examines that state with understanding, and embarks upon a scrutiny (of it).

(2) "On whatever occasion, bhikkhus, abiding thus mindful, a bhikkhu investigates, examines that state with understanding, and embarks upon a scrutiny (of it)—on that occasion the investigation-of-states enlightenment factor is aroused in him, and he develops it, and by development it comes to perfection in him.

"In him who investigates, examines that state with understanding, and embarks upon a scrutiny (of it), tireless energy is aroused.

(3) "On whatever occasion, bhikkhus, in a bhikkhu who investigates, examines that state with understanding, and embarks upon a scrutiny (of it), tireless energy is aroused—on that occasion the energy enlightenment factor is aroused in him, and he develops it, and by development it comes to perfection in him.

"In him who has aroused energy, unworldly[23] rapture arises.

(4) "On whatever occasion, bhikkhus, in a bhikkhu who has aroused energy, unworldly rapture arises—on that occasion the rapture enlightenment factor is aroused in him, and he develops it, and by development it comes to perfection in him.

"The body and mind of one whose mind is held in rapture, become tranquillized.

(5) "On whatever occasion, bhikkhus, the body and the mind of a bhikkhu whose mind is held in rapture become tranquillized—on that occasion the tranquillity enlightenment factor is aroused in him, and he develops it, and by development it comes to perfection in him.

"The mind of one who is tranquillized in body and blissful becomes concentrated.

(6) "On whatever occasion, bhikkhus, the mind of a bhikkhu who is tranquillized in body and blissful becomes concentrated—on that occasion the concentration enlightenment factor is aroused in him, and he develops it, and by development it comes to perfection in him.

"He becomes one who looks with complete equanimity on the mind thus concentrated.

(7) "On whatever occasion, bhikkhus, a bhikkhu becomes one

who looks with complete equanimity on the mind thus concentrated—on that occasion the equanimity enlightenment factor is aroused in him, and he develops it, and by development it comes to perfection in him.

B. (1)–(7) "On whatever occasion, bhikkhus, a bhikkhu abides contemplating the feelings in the feelings ..."[24]—on that occasion the equanimity enlightenment factor ... comes to perfection in him.

C. (1)–(7) "On whatever occasion, bhikkhus, a bhikkhu abides contemplating the mind in the mind ..."—on that occasion the equanimity enlightenment factor ... comes to perfection in him.

D. (1)–(7) "On whatever occasion, bhikkhus, a bhikkhu abides contemplating mental-objects in mental-objects ..."—on that occasion the equanimity enlightenment factor ... comes to perfection in him.

"Thus developed, bhikkhus, thus repeatedly practised, the four foundations of mindfulness fulfil the seven enlightenment factors.

Perfection of Clear Vision and Deliverance

"And how developed, bhikkhus, how repeatedly practised, do the seven enlightenment factors perfect clear vision and deliverance?

(1) "Here, bhikkhus, a bhikkhu develops the mindfulness enlightenment factor dependent on seclusion, on fading away, on cessation, resulting in relinquishment.

(2) "He develops the investigation-of-states enlightenment factor dependent on seclusion, on fading away, on cessation, resulting in relinquishment.

(3) "He develops the energy enlightenment factor dependent on seclusion, on fading away, on cessation, resulting in relinquishment.

(4) "He develops the rapture enlightenment factor dependent on seclusion, on fading away, on cessation, resulting in relinquishment.

(5) "He develops the tranquillity enlightenment factor dependent on seclusion, on fading away, on cessation, resulting in relinquishment.

(6) "He develops the concentration enlightenment factor dependent on seclusion, on fading away, on cessation, resulting in relinquishment.

(7) "He develops the equanimity enlightenment factor dependent on seclusion, on fading away, on cessation, resulting in relinquishment.

"Thus developed, bhikkhus, thus repeatedly practised, the seven factors of enlightenment perfect clear vision and deliverance."

So said the Blessed One. Glad at heart, the bhikkhus rejoiced at his words.

Part II

THE COMMENTARY ON THE SUTTA

(From *Visuddhimagga* and *Papañcasūdanī*)

Foreword

The commentary that follows is taken from the *Visuddhimagga* and the *Papañcasūdanī*. The only alterations made in the *Visuddhimagga*, section on respiration-mindfulness, are as follows: firstly, the *Visuddhimagga* employs as its text a parallel sutta from the Samyutta with a slightly different introduction, and this required the substitution, on p.15, of material drawn from elsewhere in the *Papañcasūdanī* (see n.1). Secondly, certain long quotations from the *Paṭisambhidāmagga* have been replaced by references, since the material quoted is given later, in the rendering of the *Paṭisambhidāmagga* itself in Part III. Such abbreviations are indicated in the notes.

The commentary on the sutta in the *Papañcasūdanī* deals only with the introduction and that part of the sutta which follows the "four tetrads"; it refers the reader to the *Visuddhimagga* for the commentary on the four tetrads. Of this, the commentary to the introduction has been omitted.

Contents

THE COMMENTARY

Introductory

1. Now the Blessed One has extolled respiration-mindfulness as a meditation subject thus: "This respiration-mindfulness concentration, bhikkhus, developed and repeatedly practised, is both peaceful and sublime, unadulterated and of happy life; it causes to vanish at once and suppresses evil, unprofitable thoughts as soon as they arise" (SN V 321). And it has been set forth as having sixteen bases in the passage beginning: **"And how developed, bhikkhus, how repeatedly practised."**

We now come to the method of its development. But since that method is only complete in all its aspects when stated in accordance with the commentary on the text, the description of its development is here preceded by the word commentary on the text.

"And how developed, bhikkhus, how repeatedly practised, is respiration-mindfulness," etc.: Here, firstly, **"How?"** is a question showing desire to expound in detail the development of respiration-mindfulness in its various aspects; **"developed, bhikkhu ... is respiration-mindfulness"** is the description of the thing asked about by the question, showing desire to expound in detail as to the various aspects. **"How repeatedly practised":** here also the method of construing is the same. Herein, **"developed"** means aroused, or increased; **"respiration-mindfulness"** means mindfulness which lays hold of respiration; or mindfulness of respiration is respiration-mindfulness; **"repeatedly practised"** means done again and again; **"is of great fruit, of great benefit"**: both these expressions are the same as to meaning, and only different in the letter; or "the fruit thereof is much mundane bliss" is "of great fruit"; and "it is the condition for great supramundane bliss" is "of great benefit." And this is the meaning in brief: "Bhikkhus, in what manner, in what way, in what sense is respiration-mindfulness developed? In what manner, being repeatedly practised, is it of great fruit, of great benefit?"

Now,[1] expounding that meaning in detail, he said, **"Here bhikkhus"** and so on. Herein, **"Here, bhikkhus, a bhikkhu"** means a bhikkhu in this dispensation. For this word "here" is the indication of the dispensation which is the prerequisite for the person who produces respiration-mindfulness concentration in all its aspects, and the denial of such a state in any other dispensation; for this is said, "Bhikkhus, only here is there a recluse, a second recluse, a third recluse, a fourth recluse; devoid of recluses are the teachings of other sectarians" (MN I 63–64).[2] Hence it was said "a bhikkhu in this dispensation."

"Gone to the forest ... or to an empty place": this indicates the acquisition of an abode favourable to the development of respiration-mindfulness concentration. For the mind of this bhikkhu, which has long been pursuing sense objects such as visible forms and so on, has no wish to mount respiration-mindfulness concentration as its object; but it runs off the track like a vehicle yoked to a vicious ox.[3] Therefore, just as a cowherd, wishing to tame a vicious calf that has been nourished by drinking the milk of a vicious cow, might take it away from the cow and tie it up alone by a rope to a strong post driven into the ground, then that calf of his, dashing to and fro, unable to run away, sits down or lies down by that post; so indeed, the bhikkhu, wishing to tame his corrupted mind, which has for long been nourished on the essence arising out of sense

objects such as visible forms and so on, and taking it to the forest,
or to the root of a tree, or to an empty place, should tie it there by
the rope of mindfulness to the post of in-and-out breathing. And so
that mind of his, though it may dash to and fro, since it no longer
obtains the object it was formerly accustomed to, being unable to
break the rope of mindfulness and run away, it sits down, lies down,
beside that object, by virtue of access and full absorption.[4] Hence
the Ancients said:

> Just as the man who tames a calf
> Would tie it to a post, so here
> Should one's own mind by mindfulness
> Be firmly fastened to the object.

Thus is such a dwelling favourable to his development. Hence
it was said above, "this indicates the acquisition of an abode favourable to the development of respiration-mindfulness concentration."

Or alternatively, because this respiration-mindfulness as a meditation subject—which is foremost among the various meditation
subjects for all Buddhas, (some)[5] Paccekebuddhas, and (some)
Buddhas' disciples, as the basis for the attainment of distinction
and a happy life here and now—is not easy to develop without
avoiding the neighbourhood of a village, which is full of the noise
of women, men, elephants, horses, etc., noise being a thorn to jhāna,[6]
whereas in the forest away from a village this meditation subject is
easily laid hold of by the yogin, who can thence produce the fourfold jhāna in respiration-mindfulness and, making that jhāna the
basis for comprehending the formations (with insight), reach the
highest fruit, arahatship—that is why, in pointing out an abode
favourable to this, the Blessed One said "gone to the forest," and
so on.

For the Blessed One is like a master of the science of building
sites.[7] As the master of the science of building sites looks over the
site for a town, examines it well, and directs, "Build the town here,"
and, when the town is safely finished, receives great honour from

the royal family; so he examines an abode as to its suitability for the yogin and directs, "Here you should devote yourself to the subject of meditation," and later on, when the yogin, by devoting himself to the subject of meditation, reaches arahatship and says, "The Blessed One is, indeed, fully enlightened," the Blessed One receives great honour.

And this bhikkhu is said to be like a leopard. For as the leopard king lurks in the forest in a grass thicket, or a woodland thicket, or a mountain thicket, and seizes wild beasts—the wild buffalo, wild ox, boar, etc.—so, too, the bhikkhu who devotes himself to the subject of meditation in the forest, etc., in due course seizes the paths of stream-entry, once-return, non-return, or arahatship, and the noble fruitions as well. Thus should it be understood. Hence the Ancients said:

> For as the leopard, by his lurking
> In the forest seizes wild beasts,
> So also will this Buddha's son
> Strenuous, with insight gifted,
> By retreating to the forest
> Seize the highest fruit of all.

Therefore, in pointing out for him the forest abode as a fitting place for advancement and rapid endeavour, the Blessed One said "gone to the forest," and so on.

Herein, **"gone to the forest"** means any kind of forest possessed of the bliss of seclusion among the kinds of forests characterized thus: "Having gone out beyond the boundary post,[8] all that is forest" (Ps I 176; *Vibhaṅga*, 251) and "a forest abode is five hundred bow-lengths distant" (Vin IV 183).

"To the root of a tree" (means) gone to the vicinity of a tree.[9]

"To an empty place": to what is an empty, secluded space. And here it is right to say that he has gone to an empty place if, besides the forest and the root of a tree (already mentioned), he goes to (one of) the remaining seven (of the nine kinds of abode).[10]

Thus having indicated an abode suitable to the three seasons,[11] suitable to humour and to temperament, and favourable to the development of respiration-mindfulness, he said, **"sits down,"** and so on, indicating a posture which is peaceful and partakes neither of idleness nor agitation. Then, showing the firmness of the sitting posture, which has the bliss that proceeds from in-and-out breathing, and is the means for laying hold of the object, he said, **"having folded his legs crosswise,"** and so on.

Herein **"crosswise"** means sitting with the thighs fully locked. **"Folded"** means fixed. **"Set his body erect,"** placing the upper part of the body erect, the eighteen back-bones each resting end to end. For the skin, flesh, and sinews of one thus seated are not bent (by inclining forward). Then those feelings which would arise in him every moment from their being bent, do not arise, the mind becomes one-pointed, the meditation subject does not collapse, but attains to growth and increase.

"Established mindfulness in front of him" (*parimukhaṃ satiṃ upaṭṭhapetvā*): having placed (*ṭhapayitvā*) mindfulness (*satiṃ*) facing the meditation subject (*kammaṭṭhān-abhimukhaṃ*). Or alternatively, *pari* has the sense of control (*pariggahattho*), *mukhaṃ* has the sense of outlet from obstruction (*niyyānattho*), and *sati* has the sense of establishing (*upaṭṭhānattho*). Hence *parimukhaṃ satiṃ* is said (Ps I 176), which is the meaning according to the *Paṭisambhidā* to be understood here, too. Herein, the meaning in brief is "having made mindfulness the outlet (from opposition, forgetfulness being thereby) controlled."

"Ever mindful he breathes in, mindful he breathes out": the bhikkhu having seated himself thus and having established mindfulness thus, not abandoning it, just mindful he breathes in, mindful he breathes out; he is one who practises mindfulness, is what is said.

First Tetrad—First Base

2. Now in order to show the different ways in which he is one who practises mindfulness, he said, **"Breathing in long,"** and so on. For in the *Paṭisambhidā,* in the analysis of the passage "mindful he breathes in, mindful he breathes out," it is said: "He is one who practises mindfulness in thirty-two ways. (1) For one who knows one-pointedness and non-distraction of mind by means of long breathing-in, mindfulness is established; by means of that mindfulness, by means of that knowledge, he is one who practises mindfulness[12] ... (up to: 32) ... For one who knows one-pointedness and non-distraction of mind by means of breathing out contemplating relinquishment, mindfulness is established; by means of that mindfulness, by means of that knowledge, he is one who practises mindfulness" (Ps I 176).

Herein, **"Breathing in long"** means producing a long in-breath. *"Assāsa"* is the breath issuing out; *"passāsa"* is the breath entering in; thus it is stated in the Vinaya commentary. But in the sutta commentaries it is the opposite way round. Herein, at the time when an infant comes forth from the mother's womb, first the wind from within goes out, and subsequently the wind from without enters in with fine dust, strikes the palate, and is extinguished (with the infant's sneezing). Thus in the first place should *assāsa* and *passāsa* be understood.[13]

But their length and shortness should be understood by way of extent. For, just as water or sand spread over an extent of space is called a long water, a long sand, a short water, a short sand; so in-breaths and out-breaths, taken in minute quantities (i.e. by way of a state of innumerable groups) in the body of an elephant and in the body of a snake, slowly fill the long extent (of space) called their physical structures and slowly go out. Therefore they are called long. They quickly fill the short extent (of space), called the physical structure of a dog, of a hare, and such creatures, and quickly go out. Therefore they are called short. And among mankind, some,

like elephant and snakes, etc., breathe in and breathe out long by
way of a long extent; others breathe in and out short like dogs and
hares, etc. Therefore (the breaths) which travel over a long extent
in entering in and going out are to be understood as long in time;
and the breaths which travel over a short extent in entering in and
going out, as short in time. Here, this bhikkhu breathing in and
breathing out long in nine ways knows, "I breathe in, I breathe out,
long." And for him who knows thus, the development of the foundation of mindfulness consisting of the contemplation of the body
should be understood to succeed in one aspect, according as it is
said in the *Paṭisambhidā* in the passage beginning, "He breathes in
a long in-breath reckoned as a long extent," and ending, "Hence it
is called, 'The development of the foundation of mindfulness consisting of contemplation of the body in the body.'"[14]

Second Base

3. So also in the case of the **short** breaths. But there is this
difference: while in the former case "a long in-breath reckoned as
a long extent" is said, here in the same context "a short in-breath
reckoned as a short extent" has been handed down. Therefore it
should be construed with the word "short" as far as the phrase
"Hence it is called, 'The development of the foundation of
mindfulness consisting of contemplation of the body in the body.'"
Thus this yogin, when understanding in-breaths and out-breaths in
these ways by way of what is reckoned as a long extent and what
is reckoned as a short extent, should be understood as **"Breathing
in long, he knows, I breathe in long; ... breathing out short, he
knows, I breathe out short."**

> The long kind and the short as well,
> The in-breath and the out-breath, too—
> Such are the four kinds that happen
> At the nose-tip of the bhikkhu—

who knows thus.

Third Base

4. **"Experiencing the whole body I shall breathe in ... shall breathe out, thus he trains himself"** means, "Making known, making plain, the beginning, middle, and end of the entire in-breath body, I shall breathe in," he trains himself; "making known, making plain, the beginning, middle, and end of the entire out-breath body, I shall breathe out," he trains himself. Thus making them known, making them plain, he both breathes in and breathes out with consciousness associated with knowledge, therefore, "I shall breathe in, I shall breathe out, thus he trains himself," is said. For to one bhikkhu, the beginning of the in-breath body or the out-breath body, diffused in minute particles,[15] is plain, but not the middle nor the end; he is able only to lay hold of the beginning and is troubled by the middle and the end. To another the middle is plain, not the beginning nor the end; he is able only to lay hold of the middle and is troubled by the beginning and the end. To another the end is plain, not the beginning nor the middle; he is able only to lay hold of the end and is troubled by the beginning and the middle. To another all stages are plain; he is able to lay hold of them all and is nowhere troubled. Pointing out that one should be like the last (mentioned), (the Blessed One) said, "Experiencing the whole body, I shall breathe in ... shall breathe out, thus he trains himself."

Herein, **"he trains himself"** (means) he strives, endeavours thus. The restraint of one so become is here the training of higher virtuous conduct; the concentration of one so become is the training of higher consciousness; the understanding of one so become is the training of higher understanding. So he trains in, cultivates, develops, repeatedly practises these three courses of training in that object, by means of that mindfulness, by means of that bringing to mind. Thus should the meaning be understood here. Herein, because in the early (stage of the) method,[16] he should only breathe in and breathe out and should not do anything else at all, and afterwards effort is to be made for the arousing of understanding, etc., consequently the present tense is used in the passage, "He knows, 'I breathe in'; he knows, 'I breathe out.'" But the future tense is used in the passages that follow, beginning with "Experiencing the whole body, I shall breathe in," in order to show how thereafter to bring about the arising of knowledge, etc. Thus it should be understood.

Fourth Base

5. **"Calming the bodily formation I shall breathe in ... shall breathe out, thus he trains himself."** "**Calming,** tranquillizing, suppressing, allaying, the gross **bodily formation,** I shall breathe in, shall breathe out," he trains himself. And here, the grossness and subtlety, and the calming are to be understood thus. For previously, at the time when he has still not discerned (the meditation subject), the body and the mind of the bhikkhu are disturbed and gross. And when the grossness of the body and mind does not subside, the in-and-out breaths, too, are gross, becoming very strong (so that) the nostrils cannot contain them and he takes to breathing through the mouth. But when his body and mind have been discerned, then they become peaceful and at rest. When they are at rest, the in-breaths and out-breaths become (so) subtle that, having reached a state of doubt (as to their existence, he asks), "Do they exist, or do they not?"

Just as the breaths of a man standing (still) after running or descending from a hill, or after putting down a heavy load from his head, are gross, and the nostrils cannot contain them and he stands breathing in and breathing out through the mouth; but when, having got rid of his fatigue and bathed and drunk and put a piece of wet-cloth on his heart, he lies in the cool shade, then his in-and-out breaths become (so) subtle that, having reached a state of doubt (as to their existence, he might ask), "Do they exist, or do they not?"—so, indeed, previously, at the time when he has still not discerned ... (and so on as above) ... having reached a state of doubt (as to their existence, he asks), "Do they exist, or do they not?" Why is this so? Because, previously, at the time when he has not discerned them, he does not think, nor lay it to heart, nor reflect, nor consider: "I am calming the grosser bodily formation," which, however, he does at the time when he has discerned them. Hence his bodily formation is subtler at the time when he has discerned them than at the time when he has not. Hence the Ancients said:

> When mind and body are disturbed,
> Then in excess it occurs;
> When the body is undisturbed,
> Then with subtlety it occurs.

In discerning[17] the formation is gross, and it is subtle in the first jhāna access; also it is gross in that (and) subtle in the first jhāna; in the first jhāna and second jhāna access it is gross, (and) in the second jhāna subtle; in the second jhāna and third jhāna access it is gross, (and) in the third jhāna subtle; in the third jhāna and fourth jhāna access it is gross, and in the fourth jhāna it is exceedingly subtle and even reaches suspension. This is the opinion of the Dīgha and Saṃyutta Reciters. But the Majjhima Reciters would have it that it is more subtle in the access than in the jhāna immediately below, (saying) "in the first jhāna it is gross, in the second jhāna access it is subtle" (and so on). It is however, the opinion of all that the occurrence of the bodily formation at the time of not discerning is tranquillized at the time of discerning; the bodily formation that arose at the time of discerning is tranquillized in the first jhāna access ... the bodily formation that arose in the fourth jhāna access is tranquillized in the fourth jhāna. This is the method in so far as concerns tranquillity.

But in so far as concerns insight, the bodily formation occurring at the time of not discerning is gross, and in discerning the great primaries[18] it is subtle; that also is gross and in discerning derived materiality[19] it is subtle; that also is gross and in discerning all materiality it is subtle; that also is gross and in discerning the

immaterial it is subtle; that also is gross and in discerning the
material and the immaterial it is subtle; that also is gross and in
discerning conditions it is subtle; that also is gross and in seeing
mentality-materiality with its conditions it is subtle; that also is
gross and in insight which has the (three) characteristics[20] as object
it is subtle; that also is gross in weak insight, and in strong insight
it is subtle.

Here, the tranquillizing of the preceding by way of (i.e., as compared with) the subsequent is to be understood according to the
method stated above.[21] Thus should grossness and subtlety, as well
as calming, be understood here. But the meaning is stated in the
Paṭisambhidā together with objection and reply (and the simile of
the gong).[22] This in the first place is the consecutive commentary
on the first tetrad which is stated by way of contemplation of the
body.

METHOD OF PRACTICE

Learning

6. The first tetrad is stated as a meditation subject for a beginner; but the other three tetrads are (respectively) stated by way of
contemplation of the feelings, the mind, and mental objects for one
who has attained the first jhāna. So if a clansman who is a beginner desires, by developing the meditation subject, to reach arahatship
together with analysis[23] by means of insight which has as its basis
fourfold jhāna due to respiration-mindfulness, he should first per-
form all the functions of purifying virtue,[24] etc., in the way described in the *Visuddhimagga*, and he should then set about learning the meditation subject in five stages from a teacher of the kind
described in the *Visuddhimagga* (III 61–65).

These are the five stages herein: learning, questioning, establishing, absorption, and characteristic. Herein, "learning" is the learning of the meditation subject; "questioning" is the questioning about
the meditation subject; "establishing" is the establishing of the

meditation subject; "absorption" is the absorption in the meditation subject; "characteristic" is the characteristic of the meditation subject—"the recognition of the nature of the meditation subject (by knowing) 'this meditation subject has such a characteristic,' " is what is meant. Learning in this way in five stages he does not tire himself or worry the teacher. Therefore, he should learn a little at a time and take a long time reciting it. While learning the meditation subject in the five stages thus, he may live either with the teacher or in an abode of the sort already described in the *Visuddhimagga* (IV 19).

The Start of Practice

So, after he has got rid of the minor impediments,[25] done all his duties, and dispelled drowsiness due to eating,[26] he should seat himself comfortably. He should then gladden the mind by reflecting on the qualities of the Three Jewels,[27] and then set himself to bring to his mind this respiration-mindfulness as his meditation subject, after he has assured himself that he is not in doubt about any part of the lesson learnt from the teacher.[28]

The Stages of Practice

Herein, these are the stages in giving attention to it: (1) counting, (2) connection, (3) contact, (4) fixing, (5) observing, (6) turning away, (7) purification, and (8) the looking back on these. Herein, "counting" is just counting; "connection" is carrying on; "contact" is the place touched (by the breaths); "fixing" is absorption; "observing" is insight; "turning away" is the path; "purification" is fruition; "the looking back on these" is reviewing.[29]

Counting[30]

Herein, the clansman who is a beginner should first give attention to this meditation subject by counting. And when counting he should not stop short of five nor go beyond ten, neither should he make any break in the series (such as counting "one, three, five"[31]). In one who stops short of five, consciousness, being arisen in a confined space, is restless like a herd of cattle shut in a pen. In one who goes beyond ten, consciousness comes to depend on the number (instead of the breath). The mind of one who breaks the series vacillates, and he wonders, "Has the subject of meditation reached completion or not?" Therefore he should count, avoiding these faults. At first he should count slowly (that is, late) after the manner of a grain-measurer. For a grain-measurer, having filled his basket and said "one," empties it. And, refilling it, he says, "One, one," while removing any rubbish he may have noticed. And the same with "Two, two," and so forth. So, seizing that breath which becomes manifest thus from among the in-breaths and out-breaths,[32] he should begin counting, "One, one," and go on till he has counted "Ten, ten," noting the occurrence all the time (of the uninterrupted in-and-out breathing).[33] By thus counting, his in-and-out breaths entering in and issuing out become evident (to him, because of the absence of external distraction).[34]

Then, when he has finished counting slowly (late) like a grain-measurer, he should count quickly (that is, early) like a cowherd. For a skilled cowherd takes pebbles, etc., in his pocket and goes early to the cowpen, whip in hand, where he sits on the crossbar (of the gate); he taps the cows on the back and counts them as they reach the gate, dropping a stone for each one saying, "one, two." And the cows of the herd, which have been spending the three watches of the night uncomfortably in the cramped space, come out quickly in groups, jostling each other in going out. So he counts quickly (early), "three, four, five … ten." Thus the in-breaths and out-breaths, which have become evident to him by counting in the former (slow) way, now come and go quickly and continuously. Then, knowing that they come and go continuously, not seizing them either inside or outside (the body) but seizing them just as they reach the (nostril) door, he can do his counting quickly (early): one, two, three, four, five; one, two, three, four, five, six; one, two,

three, four, five, six, seven; ... eight; ... nine; ... ten.[35] For when
the meditation subject is connected with counting, it is with the
help of that very counting that the mind becomes one-pointed, just
as a boat in a swift current is steadied with the help of a rudder.
When he counts quickly (early), the meditation subject becomes
apparent to him as an uninterrupted process. Then, knowing that it
proceeds without interruption, without discerning the breath either
inside or outside (the body), he can count quickly in the way already described. For, by bringing his consciousness inside along
with the incoming breath, it seems as if it were buffeted by the
wind inside or filled with fat.[36] By taking his consciousness outside together with the outgoing breath it gets distracted among the
many objects outside. However, his development is successful when
he fixes his mindfulness on the place of contact.[37]

But how long is he to go on counting? Until, without counting,
mindfulness is thoroughly established in the in-breaths and out-
breaths as objects. For counting, by cutting off thoughts which cling
to external things, serves the purpose of establishing mindfulness
in the in-breaths and out-breaths as object. Having given attention
to it by counting, he should now do so by means of connection.[38]

Connection

Connection is the uninterrupted following of the in-breaths and
out-breaths with mindfulness, after giving up counting. And that is
not by following the beginning, middle, and end.[39] Of the breath
issuing out, the navel is the beginning, the heart the middle, the
nose-tip the end.[40] Of the breath entering in, the nose-tip is the
beginning, the heart the middle, and the navel the end. And the
mind of one who follows the breathing (through the three places)
is confused by agitation and vacillation, according as is said in the
Paṭisambhidā: "In one whose consciousness is distracted internally
by following with mindfulness the beginning, middle, and end of
the in-breath, both body and mind are disturbed, unsettled, and

unsteady. In one whose consciousness is distracted externally by following with mindfulness the beginning, middle, and end of the out-breath, both body and mind are disturbed, unsettled, and unsteady." [41] So when he gives his attention to it by connection he should do so not by the beginning, middle, and end, but rather by contact and by fixing.

Contact and Fixing [42]

There is, in fact, no attention to be given to it by contact separate from fixing, as there is by counting separate from connection.[43] In counting the breath at the point of contact, however, he brings them to mind by way of counting and contact; after giving up counting them just there at the point of contact, when connecting them by means of mindfulness, and fixing consciousness by means of absorption, he is said to be giving his attention to them by connection, contact, and fixing. And the meaning of this is to be understood after the similes of the lame man and the gate-keeper, as stated in the commentaries, and by the simile of the saw in the *Paṭisambhidā*.

The Similes

Of these, this is the simile of the lame man: Just as a lame man, in rocking a swing for the amusement of his family, sits at the foot of the swing post and sees both ends and the middle of the swing plank coming and going, yet does not move from his place to see the two ends and the middle; so, indeed, the bhikkhu, having placed himself by means of mindfulness at the foot of the post of connection, and rocking the swing of the in-breaths and out-breaths; and sitting just there at the sign of mindfulness (i.e. the nose-tip),[44] following with mindfulness the beginning, middle, and end[45] of the in-breaths and out-breaths coming and going successively at the point of contact, fixing his mind there, he then sees them, without moving from his place in order to see them. This is the simile of the lame man.

And this is the simile of the gate-keeper: Just as a gate-keeper does not examine people inside and outside the town, (asking) "Who are you? Where have you come from? Where are you going? What have you got in your hand?"—for these people are not his concern—but he examines each man as he arrives at the gate; so, indeed, the incoming breaths inside and the outgoing breaths outside are not the concern of this bhikkhu but, as they arrive just at the gate (of the nostril), they are his concern.

But the simile of the saw should here be understood from the beginning thus. For this is said:

> Sign, in-breath, out-breath, are not object
> Of a single consciousness;
> By one who knows not these three things,
> Development is not obtained.

> Sign, in-breath, out-breath, are not object
> Of a single consciousness;
> By one who does know these three things,
> Development will be obtained.

"How is it that these things are not the object of a single consciousness, that they are nevertheless not unknown, that the mind does not become distracted, that he manifests effort, carries out a task, and achieves an effect?

"It is as though a man were to cut with a saw a tree trunk placed on level ground. His mindfulness is established by the teeth of the saw at the point where they come into contact with the tree trunk, without his giving attention to the teeth of the saw as they approach and recede, although he is not unaware of these; and he manifests endeavour, accomplishes the task, and achieves distinction.

"As the tree trunk on the level ground, so the sign for the binding (of mindfulness). As the teeth of the saw, so the in-breaths and out-breaths. As the man's mindfulness is established by the teeth

of the saw at the point where they come into contact with the tree
trunk, without his giving attention to the teeth of the saw as they
approach and recede, although he is not unaware of these, so he
manifests endeavour, accomplishes the task, and achieves distinction—so, indeed, the bhikkhu sits, having established his mindfulness at the nose-tip or on the upper lip, without giving attention to
the in-breaths and out-breaths as they approach and recede, although
he is not unaware of these, and he manifests endeavour, accomplishes the task, and achieves distinction.

"The body and the mind of one who is energetic become pliable
—this is the endeavour. The imperfections of one who is energetic
are abandoned and his applied thinking is pacified—this is the task.
The fetters of one who is energetic are abandoned and his inherent
tendencies are brought to an end—this is the distinction. Thus these
three things are not the object of a single consciousness, nor are
these three things unknown, nor does consciousness become
distracted; he manifests endeavour, accomplishes the task, and
achieves distinction.

> Whose mindfulness of breathing in
> And out is perfect, well developed,
> Gradually brought to growth
> According as the Buddha taught,
> 'Tis he illuminates the world,
> Like the full moon freed from cloud.

This is the simile of the saw (Ps I 170). But here its purpose
should be understood as the mere non-attending to the coming and
going (of breaths).[46]

The Sign [47]

When someone gives his attention to this subject of meditation,
sometimes it is not long before the sign[48] arises in him and then the
fixing called absorption adorned with the remaining jhāna factors[49]

is achieved. But when anyone's physical disturbance is quieted by the gradual cessation of gross in-and-out breathing since the time of giving attention to it by counting, both body and mind become light as though the body would leap up into the air. Just as, when a body which is disturbed sits down on a bed or chair, the bed or chair sags down and creaks, and the cover becomes rumpled. But when a body which is not disturbed sits down, the bed or chair neither sags down nor creaks, nor does the cover become rumpled, but the bed or chair is as though filled with cotton wool. Why? Because a body which is not disturbed is light. So, when physical disturbance has been stilled by the gradual cessation of the gross in-and-out breathing since attention has been given to counting, both body and mind become light as though the body would spring up into the sky.

When his gross in-and-out breathing has ceased, consciousness occurs with the sign of the subtle in-and-out breathing as object. And when this has ceased, it occurs having the successively more and more subtle sign as object. How? Suppose a man strikes a metal gong with a big iron rod and a loud sound results simultaneously, his consciousness occurs with the gross sound as object; and when afterwards the gross sound has ceased, then consciousness has the sign of the subtle sound as object; and when this has ceased, it occurs having the sign of the more and more subtle sound as object. And this is given in detail in the passage beginning "just as when a metal gong is struck" (Ps I 184).

While other subjects of meditation become clearer at each higher stage, this one does not. But for him who is developing it, it becomes more subtle at each higher stage. Also it comes to the point at which it is not manifested. But, when it is not manifested thus, the bhikkhu should not rise from his seat and go away shaking his leather mat. What should be done? He should not rise with the idea, "Shall I ask the teacher?" or "Is my meditation subject lost?" For, by going away and so disturbing his posture, the meditation subject becomes new again (and has to be begun afresh). Therefore, by just sitting as he was, it should be reinstated from the point (of contact—the nose-tip where it was formerly established).[50]

This is the means by which he brings it back: The bhikkhu, recognizing the state of non-manifestation of the meditation subject, should consider thus: "Where are these in-and-out breaths? Where are they not? Whose are they? Whose are they not?" Then, considering thus (and) recognizing that they are not in one within the mother's womb, nor in those who are drowned in water, nor similarly in unconscious beings, in the dead, in those who have entered into the fourth jhāna, in those endowed with existence in the fine-material or immaterial states, nor in those who have entered into the attainment of cessation—he should apostrophize himself thus: "You, with all your wisdom, are certainly (none of these). Those in-breaths and out-breaths are, in fact, existent in you but you cannot grasp them owing to the slowness of your perception." Then, fixing his mind by means of the original point of contact, he should proceed to give his attention to that. For these (in-breaths and out-breaths) for a long-nosed man occur striking the tip of the nose, and for a short-nosed man the upper lip. Therefore, the sign should be fixed, knowing, "They strike this place."

It was for this reason that the Blessed One said: "I do not say, bhikkhus, that there is development of respiration-mindfulness in one who is forgetful and does not clearly comprehend" (see p.8). For although any meditation subject succeeds only for one who is mindful and clearly comprehending, any subject other than this becomes more evident as he goes on giving it his attention. But this respiration-mindfulness as a subject of meditation is difficult, difficult to develop, and a field in which only the minds of Buddhas, Paccekabuddhas, and Buddhas' sons are at home. It is no trivial matter, nor can it be cultivated by trivial persons. In proportion as continued attention is given to it, it becomes more peaceful and more subtle; therefore, strong mindfulness and understanding are needed here. For, as in doing needlework on a piece of fine cloth it is necessary that the needle should be fine, too, and the instrument for boring the needle's eye still finer; so, while developing this subject of meditation, which is like fine cloth, it is necessary that both mindfulness, which is like the needle, and understanding associated therewith, which is like the instrument that bores the needle's eye, should be strong. And the bhikkhu who is possessed of this mindfulness and understanding should not look for these in-breaths and out-breaths elsewhere than at the original place of contact.

Just as a farmer, who has ploughed his field and has unyoked his oxen and let them go to pasture, might rest himself, sitting in the shade; and his oxen go quickly into the woods. A practical farmer, who wishes to catch them and yoke them again, does not wander in the forest following their tracks, but goes straight with his rope and goad to the drinking place where they meet, and there he sits or lies (and waits). Then, after the oxen have roamed the whole day and come down to the drinking place where they meet and when they have bathed and drunk and come out of the water again, he ties them with his rope and, urging them on with his goad, brings them along and yokes them and resumes his work. Thus, indeed, the bhikkhu should not seek the in-breaths and out-breaths elsewhere than at the original point of contact, and taking the rope of mindfulness and the goad of understanding, he should set the mind on the original place of contact and keep that before his mind. For as he gives his attention in this way, they reappear before long, like the oxen at the drinking place where they meet. And then, fixing them with the rope of mindfulness and yoking them there and urging them on with the goad of understanding, he should repeatedly apply himself to the subject of meditation.

As he applies himself the sign[51] is established before long. But this is not the same for all. It appears to some producing a soft touch like a tuft of cotton, or silk, or like a breeze, so some say. But this is the definition in the commentaries: that the sign appears to some like a star, a round gem, or a round pearl; to some it has a harsh touch like cotton seed, or a peg made of heartwood; to some it is like a long string, or a wreath of flowers, or a puff of smoke;

to others it is like a stretched out cobweb, a film of cloud, a lotus flower, a cart-wheel, the disc of the moon, or the disc of the sun.

And, indeed, when a number of bhikkhus are seated together reciting a suttanta text, one of them asks, "Like what does the suttanta appear to you?", and one answers, "To me it appears like a great mountain torrent," and another, "To me it is like a row of forest trees," and another, "To me it is like a fruit-tree covered with foliage, giving cool shade." For one sutta appears differently to them, owing to a difference in perception. Thus the meditation subject appears variously owing to a difference in perception, for it is born of perception, originated by perception, sprung from perception. Therefore it should be understood to appear differently owing to a difference in perception.

And here, consciousness with in-breathing as object is one consciousness, with out-breathing as object is another, consciousness with the sign is a third. For one who has not these three states, the meditation subject reaches neither full absorption nor access. But for one who has these three states, the meditation subject reaches both access and full absorption. For this is said:

> Sign, in-breath, out-breath, are not object
> Of a single consciousness;
> By one who knows not these three things,
> Development is not obtained.

> Sign, in-breath, out-breath, are not object
> Of a single consciousness;
> By one who does know these three things,
> Development will be obtained.

(Ps I 170)

And when the sign has appeared, the bhikkhu should approach the teacher and inform him thus: "To me, venerable sir, such and such has appeared." The teacher should not say, "It is the sign," or, "It is not the sign," but he should say, "Friend, thus it is, go on giving it attention again and again." Were he to say, "It is the sign," (the bhikkhu, feeling complacent)[52] might become slack; were he to say, "It is not the sign," (the bhikkhu) being discouraged, might become dejected. Therefore, without saying either, he should exhort him to keep giving attention to it. So say the Dīgha Reciters. But the Majjhima Reciters hold that the teacher should say: "Friend, it is the sign. Well done. Keep giving attention to it again and again." After this (the bhikkhu) should fix the mind on the sign. Such is the development by way of fixing the mind from the time of the manifestation of the sign. For this has been said by the Ancients:

> Fixing his mind upon the sign[53]
> And putting away the various aspects,
> The clever man his own mind binds
> Onto the breathings in and out.[54]

Thus, on the establishment of the sign, his hindrances are brought to an end, his defilements are got under control, mindfulness is established, and the mind is concentrated by means of access.

Observing, etc.

After this, he should not bring the sign to mind as to colour nor consider it as to characteristic. But as the king's chief queen guards the embryo of a Wheel-turning Monarch,[55] and the farmer guards the ripening corn and crops, so he should guard the sign carefully, avoiding the kind of abode, etc., which are the seven unsuitable things, and observing the seven suitable things.[56]

Then, guarding it thus carefully, he should make it grow and improve it with repeated attention, and he should accomplish the tenfold skill in full absorption[57] and strive for evenness of energy. For one thus endeavouring, fourfold and fivefold jhāna is produced in the sign.[58] But here the bhikkhu who possesses fourfold and fivefold jhāna, and who wishes, by increasing the subject of meditation through observing and turning away, to attain to purifica-

tion, practises that same jhāna in the five way[59] until he has famil-
iarized himself with it, and establishes insight by defining mentality-materiality.

How? Rising from his attainment, he sees that the physical body
and the mind are the origin of the in-and-out breathing. For, just as
when a blacksmith's bellows are blown, wind is set in motion due
to the bellows and the man's appropriate effort; so, due to the body
and the mind, there is in-and-out breathing. Thereupon he defines
the in-breaths and out-breaths and the body as materiality, and the
mind and mental concomitant states associated therewith as the
immaterial (mind).[60] Here this is stated in brief. The definition of
mind and matter is given (in the *Visuddhimagga*, Chap. XVIII).

His doubts[61] being overcome, he attributes the three characteristics[62] (to mentality and materiality), comprehending (them) by
groups;[63] he abandons the ten corruptions of insight beginning with
illumination,[64] which arise in the first stages of the contemplation
of rise and fall; and he defines as "the path" the knowledge of the
way that is free from these corruptions. He reaches contemplation
of dissolution by abandoning (attention to) arising. When all formations have appeared as terror owing to the contemplation of their
incessant dissolution, he becomes dispassionate towards them, the
greed for them fades away, and he is liberated from them.

Having thus reached the four noble paths in due course, and
being established in the fruition of arahatship, having arrived finally
at reviewing knowledge of the nineteen various kinds,[65] he becomes
a fit person to receive the highest gifts from the world with its
deities.

At this point, the development of respiration-mindfulness concentration, beginning with "counting" and ending with "looking
back" (see p.25), is completed. Because there is no separate method
of developing the subject of meditation in the other tetrads, the
meaning of these is to be understood according to the word-by-
word commentary.

Second Tetrad

7. "**Experiencing rapture**": "making rapture known, plain, I shall breathe in, I shall breathe out, thus he trains himself." Herein, rapture is experienced in two ways: as object and as non-delusion. How is rapture experienced as object? He enters into the first two jhānas in which rapture is present. Owing to his obtaining of jhāna, at the moment of attaining it, rapture is experienced by him as object, because of the experiencing of the object. How as non-delusion? Having entered into the two jhānas in which rapture is present, and emerged therefrom, he masters the rapture associated with jhāna (by contemplating it) as destructible and perishable. By his penetration of its characteristics at the moment of insight, rapture is experienced by him as non-delusion.[66] For this is said in the *Paṭisambhidā*: "For one who knows one-pointedness and non-distraction of mind through breathing in long, mindfulness is established. By means of that mindfulness and that knowledge that rapture is experienced. For one who knows one-pointedness and non-distraction of mind through breathing out long ... breathing in short ... breathing out short ... breathing in, experiencing the whole body ... breathing out, experiencing the whole body ... breathing in, calming the bodily formation ... breathing out, calming the bodily formation, mindfulness is established. By means of that mindfulness and that knowledge that rapture is experienced. It is experienced by one who adverts, who knows, who sees, who reflects, who mentally decides, who resolves with faith, who exerts energy, who establishes mindfulness, who concentrates the mind, who understands through understanding, who directly knows what is to be directly known, who fully knows what is to be fully known, who abandons what is to be abandoned, who develops what is to be developed, who realizes what is to be realized. Thus is that rapture experienced" (Ps I 187).

The remaining expressions (in this tetrad) should be understood according to the same method as to meaning. But here this is the difference: **"experiencing bliss"** should be understood by way of three jhānas, and **"experiencing the mental formation"** is by way of four.[67] The mental formation is the two aggregates, feeling and perception. And here, as regards the expression **"experiencing bliss,"** (when it is said) in the *Paṭisambhidā* (Ps I 188) "'**Bliss**': there are two (kinds of) bliss, bodily bliss and mental bliss," that is said for the purpose of showing the plane of insight.[68]

"Calming the mental formation" means calming the gross mental formation, causing it to cease; and this is to be understood in detail in the same way as in (the case of) the bodily formation. Moreover, here, as regards the term "rapture," feeling is stated under the heading of rapture; in the term, "bliss," it is stated in its own form.[69] As regards the two phrases where "mental formation" occurs, feeling is stated as being associated with perception from the statement: "perception and feeling ... being mental properties, these things are bound up with the mind (and are) mind functions" (MN I 301). Thus this tetrad is to be understood as stated by way of contemplation of feeling.

Third Tetrad

8. In the third tetrad, **"experiencing the mind"** should be understood to be through the four jhānas.[70]

"Gladdening the mind": "heartening, gladdening, pleasing, delighting the mind, I shall breathe in, I shall breathe out, he trains himself." Herein, there is **gladdening** in two ways: through concentration and through insight. How through concentration? He enters into the two jhānas in which rapture is present. At the moment of entry he pleases, rejoices the mind with the associated rapture. How through insight? He enters into the two jhānas in which rapture is present and, emerging therefrom, contemplates the rapture associated with them as destructible and perishable. Thus, at the moment of insight, having made rapture associated with jhāna the object, he pleases, rejoices the mind. Of one practising thus it is said: "Gladdening the mind, I shall breathe in ... breathe out, thus he trains himself."

"Concentrating the mind" means centring the mind evenly, placing it evenly on the object by means of the first jhāna, and so on. Or, having entered those jhānas and risen therefrom, in one who sees the mind associated with jhāna as destructible and per- ishable, there arises, by means of penetration of the characteristics, momentary one-pointedness of mind at the moment of insight. Of one centring the mind evenly, placing it evenly on the object by means of the momentary one-pointedness of mind thus risen, it is said: "Concentrating the mind, I shall breathe in ... breathe out, thus he trains himself."

"Liberating the mind": by means of the first jhāna setting free,[71] releasing, the mind from the hindrances; by means of the second jhāna, from applied and sustained thought; by means of the third, from rapture; by means of the fourth, setting free, releasing, the mind from pleasure and pain. Or, entering into those jhānas and rising therefrom, he contemplates the consciousness associated with jhāna as destructible and perishable. At the moment of insight he breathes in and breathes out, setting free, releasing the mind from the perception of permanence by means of the contemplation of impermanence, from the perception of pleasure by means of the contemplation of pain, from the perception of self by means of the contemplation of non-self, from delight by means of the contem- plation of revulsion, from passion by means of the contemplation of dispassion (fading away), from origination by means of the con- templation of cessation; setting free, releasing the mind from clinging by means of the contemplation of relinquishment. Hence it is said: "Liberating the mind, I shall breathe in ... shall breathe out, thus he trains himself." Thus this tetrad should be understood as stated, by way of contemplation of the mind.

Fourth Tetrad

9. But as regards the fourth tetrad, here firstly, **"Contemplating impermanence"** means that the impermanent should be understood, impermanence should be understood, contemplation of impermanence should be understood, and one contemplating impermanence should be understood. Here, "impermanent" are the five aggregates. Why? Because of their rise and fall and change. "Impermanence" is just their rise and fall and change. Or it is their being no more after coming to be. The meaning is that things that are in a process of becoming, by not persisting in that quality, break up in momentary dissolution. "Contemplation of impermanence" is the contemplation of that "materiality, etc., as impermanent by reason of that impermanence." "One contemplating impermanence" is one possessed of that contemplation. Therefore, such a one breathing in and breathing out should be understood here thus: "Contemplating impermanence, I shall breathe in … shall breathe out, thus he trains himself."[72]

"Contemplating fading away": here also there are two kinds of **fading away**: fading away as destruction and absolute fading away. Herein, fading away as destruction is the momentary dissolution of formations; absolute fading away is Nibbāna. Contemplation of fading away is insight and the path which occur as seeing both kinds.[73] And one who breathes in and breathes out possessed of that twofold contemplation should be understood as "Contemplating fading away, I shall breathe in … shall breathe out, thus he trains himself."[74]

So also as regards the phrase **"Contemplating cessation."**[75]

As regards **"Contemplating relinquishment,"** here **relinquishment** is of two kinds: relinquishment as giving up, and relinquishment as entering into. Relinquishment itself as contemplation is contemplation of relinquishment;[76] this is a name for insight and the path. For insight gives up defilements together with kamma-accumulations of the aggregates by substituting for them opposite qualities; and through seeing the unsatisfactoriness of what is formed and through inclining towards its opposite, Nibbāna, it enters into it; so it is called both relinquishment as giving up and relinquishment as entering into. The path gives up defilements together with kamma-accumulations of the aggregates by means of cutting them off; by making it the object, it enters into Nibbāna; so it is called both relinquishment as giving up and relinquishment as entering into. And both of these are called contemplation because of successive contemplation of previous knowledge. And one who breathes in and breathes out possessed of that twofold contemplation of relinquishment, should be understood as "Contemplating relinquishment, I shall breathe in ... shall breathe out, thus he trains himself."[77]

This tetrad is stated by way of pure insight only. But the preceding three are by way of tranquillity and insight. So, by way of the four tetrads, should the development of respiration-mindfulness with its sixteen bases be understood.

Four Tetrads—Conclusion

10. Thus by way of the sixteen bases this respiration-mindfulness is **"of great fruit, of great benefit."** Herein its great beneficialness should be understood also by way of the state of peace from the passage beginning, "and this respiration-mindfulness concentration, bhikkhus, developed and repeatedly practised, is peaceful and sublime" (SN V 321). And also by way of cutting off applied thought; for this concentration, because it is peaceful, sublime, unadulterated and of happy living, keeps the mind on the respiration as object by cutting off the chasing here and there of the mind with applied thoughts that cause hindrance. Hence it is also said, "Respiration-mindfulness should be developed for the cutting off of applied thought" (AN IV 353).[78]

By its being the root condition in the fulfilment of clear vision and deliverance, it is also greatly beneficial. For it is said by the

Blessed One, **"Respiration-mindfulness, bhikkhus, developed and repeatedly practised, perfects the four foundations of mindfulness; the four foundations of mindfulness, developed and repeatedly practised, perfect the seven enlightenment factors; the seven enlightenment factors, developed and repeatedly practised, perfect clear vision and deliverance"** (see p.5).

Moreover, it is greatly beneficial because it causes the final breathings to be known. For this has been said by the Blessed One: "When, Rāhula, respiration-mindfulness is thus developed, thus repeatedly practised, the final in-breaths and out-breaths (are) known (when) they cease, not unknown" (MN I 425–26). Herein, there are three (kinds of breathing which are) final because of cessation: final in existence, final in jhāna, final in dying. For, among the (various planes of) existence, in-breaths and out-breaths occurs in the realm of sense-existence, (but) not in the realms of fine-material and immaterial existence; therefore, they are (called) final in existence. In the jhānas, they occur in the first three (but) not in the fourth; therefore, they are called final in jhāna. Those that arise with the sixteenth consciousness preceding decease-consciousness, cease with the decease-consciousness; they are called final in dying. It is these last that are meant here by "final." They are clear to the bhikkhu who is devoted to this meditation subject because of his thorough laying hold of respiration as object. At the moment of the arising of the sixteenth consciousness preceding decease-consciousness, to him who adverts to arising, their arising is also clear; to him who adverts to presence, their presence is also clear; and to him who adverts to dissolution, their dissolution is also clear.

A bhikkhu who has attained to arahatship, after developing some other meditation subject than this, may or may not be able to determine his life-term. But after developing respiration-mindfulness with its sixteen bases, he is able to do so. He knows, "for so long and no more will my life now continue." And, minding all the usual functions such as seeing to the needs of the body, wearing the inner and outer garments, he closes his eyes like the Elder

Tissa who lived at Kotapabbata Monastery, like Mahā-Tissa, the elder of Mahā-Karañjiya Monastery, Piṇḍapātika-Tissa, the elder in the kingdom of Devaputta, and the two brothers, elders of Cittalapabbata Monastery.

Herein, to relate one of these stories: it seems that one of the two brothers, after reciting the Pātimokkha on the full-moon assembly day, went to his own dwelling with a number of bhikkhus. As he stood on the terrace walk looking at the moonlight, he considered the span of his life and said to the bhikkhus: "How, hitherto, have you seen bhikkhus attaining complete extinction?" Some answered: "Hitherto, we have seen them attaining complete extinction sitting in their seats"; others answered: "We have seen them seated cross-legged in the sky." The elder said: "I will now show you an attaining of complete extinction while walking to and fro on the terrace." He then drew a line across the terrace walk, saying: "I shall go from here to the other end of the terrace and turn back; when I reach this line, I shall attain complete extinction." So saying, he went down the terrace to the far end and, as he returned, he attained complete extinction at the moment in which he set foot upon the line.[79]

Perfection of the Four Foundations of Mindfulness

11. **"A certain body": I say it is a certain one of the four bodies beginning with the earth body;** I say it is the air body,[80] is the meaning. Or alternatively, the twenty-five parts of (derived) materiality, namely, "visible-object base ... material nutriment," are called the materiality body. Among these, breathing, because of being included in the tangible-object base, is a certain body. That is why he spoke thus.

"That is why": because he contemplates a certain air body among the four bodies, or a certain breathing in the materiality body of twenty-five parts, that is why he **"abides contemplating the body in the body,"** is the meaning. So should the meaning be understood throughout.

"A certain feeling": this is said with reference to pleasant feeling as a certain one among the three feelings.[81]

"The giving attention completely": the full attention arisen through the experiencing of rapture, etc. But how? Is attention pleasant feeling? It is not. But this is a heading of the teaching. Just as, in the phrase, "devoted to the practice of perception of impermanence" (see p.5 above), by the word "perception" understanding is there stated; so here also, by the expression "attention," feeling should be understood to be stated. For in this tetrad, in the first phrase feeling is stated under the heading of rapture, and in the second phrase it is stated in its own nature as bliss. In the two phrases dealing with the mental formation, because of the passage which says, "Perception and feeling are mental, these states being bound up with the mind are mental formations" (MN I 301); and because of the passage which says, "Excepting applied and sustained thought, also all states associated with consciousness are included in the mental formation," feeling is stated by the word "formation." Including all that with the phrase "attention," he here said, "The giving attention completely."

Then, this being so, because this feeling is not the object, is the expression "contemplating the feelings" therefore incorrect? It is not incorrect. For also in the commentary to the Satipaṭṭhāna Sutta it is said, "feeling feels by making this or that basis of pleasure, and so on, the object; but the words 'I feel' are merely a conventional expression used with regard to the occurrence of that feeling" (Paps I 275). Furthermore, this method of deduction is given, too, in the commentary, on the meaning of "experiencing rapture," and so on. For this is said in the *Visuddhimagga* (see p.37 above), "Herein rapture is experienced in two ways, as object and as non-delusion. How is rapture experienced as object? He enters into the first two jhānas in which rapture is present. Owing to his obtaining of jhāna, at the moment of attaining it, rapture is experienced by him as object, because of the experiencing of the object. How as non-delusion? Having entered into the two jhānas in which rapture is present, and emerged therefrom, he masters the rapture associated with jhāna (by contemplating it) as destructible and perishable. By his penetration of its characteristics at the moment of insight, rapture is experienced by him as non-delusion. For this is said in the *Paṭisambhidā*: 'For one who knows one-pointedness and non-distraction of mind through breathing in long, mindfulness is established. By means of that mindfulness and that knowledge that rapture is experienced ...' (Ps I 187). The remaining expressions (in this tetrad) should be understood according to the same method as to meaning." Accordingly, just as rapture, bliss, and the mental formation are experienced as object through the obtaining of jhāna, so feeling is experienced as non-delusion through the obtaining of this attention called feeling which is associated with jhāna. Therefore, this passage, **"on that occasion ... a bhikkhu abides contemplating the feelings in the feelings"** is rightly stated.

"One who is forgetful and does not clearly comprehend": here this is the intention: a bhikkhu who proceeds by the method, "Experiencing the mind, I shall breathe in," etc., although he makes the sign of the in-and-out breathing the object, is nevertheless called "one who experiences the mind," owing to the proceeding of his mind thus only after establishing mindfulness and clear comprehension in regard to the object. For there is no development of respiration-mindfulness in one who is forgetful and not clearly comprehending. That is why, by experiencing the mind, etc., as object, **"on that occasion ... a bhikkhu abides contemplating the mind in the mind."**

"Having seen with understanding what is the abandoning of covetousness and grief, he becomes one who looks on with complete equanimity": here "covetousness" is the hindrance of lust. By "grief" the hindrance of ill will is pointed out. For this tetrad is stated by way of insight. And contemplation of mental objects is sixfold in the section beginning with contemplation on the hindrances (see MN No. 10, Contemplation of Mental Objects). Of that contemplation, the section on the hindrances is the beginning.

Accordingly, he said, "covetousness and grief" in order to point out the beginning of contemplation of mental objects. "The abandoning" means it is the knowledge of abandoning, thus, "He abandons the perception of permanence through the contemplation of impermanence," that is intended. "Having seen with understanding what is," means having seen by means of further insight-understanding that knowledge of abandoning which is called knowledge of impermanence, fading away, cessation, and relinquishment, and having seen that also by means of further insight-understanding thus he points out successive insight. "He becomes one who looks on with complete equanimity," means he looks with equanimity on what has arrived at tranquillity,[82] and he looks with equanimity on what is establishment as one—thus he looks on with equanimity in two ways. Herein, there is looking with equanimity on conascent states, and looking with equanimity on the object, that is intended. **"That is why ... bhikkhus"**: because one who proceeds by the method, "contemplating impermanence, I shall breathe in," etc., is one who looks on with complete equanimity after successively seeing with understanding not only the mental objects beginning with the hindrances,[83] but also the knowledge of the abandoning of the mental objects stated under the heading of covetousness and grief. Therefore, it should be understood that **"on that occasion ... a bhikkhu abides contemplating mental objects in mental objects."**

The Seven Enlightenment Factors

12. **"He investigates"**: he investigates by way of impermanence, etc.; the other two phrases are synonyms for this.

"Unworldly": free from defilements.

"Tranquillized": through the tranquillization of bodily and mental disturbance, the body and the mind become tranquillized.

"Becomes concentrated": calm is established; it becomes as though attained to full absorption.

"He becomes one who looks on with complete equanimity": he becomes one who looks on with equanimity by means of looking on with equanimity which is conascent. The mindfulness in regard to the body, in the bhikkhu who lays hold of the body in the fourteen ways (of contemplating the body, given in the Satipaṭṭhāna Sutta) thus, is the **mindfulness enlightenment factor;** the knowledge associated with that is the **investigation-of-states** enlightenment factor; the bodily and mental energy associated with that is the **energy** enlightenment factor, (and so on in like manner with) **rapture** and **tranquillity;** one-pointedness is the **concentration** enlightenment factor; it is the quality of equipoise called absence of lagging behind or of overrunning on the part of the aforesaid six enlightenment factors, that constitutes the **equanimity** enlightenment factor. For just as, when the horses are advancing evenly, there is on the charioteer's part no urging on, (saying), "This one is holding back"; nor holding in, saying, "This one is overrunning"; but only the static quality of one watching thus: so, indeed, it is the quality of equipoise called absence of lagging behind or of overrunning in these six enlightenment factors that constitutes the equanimity enlightenment factor.

Up to this point what has been expounded? What are expounded are the **seven enlightenment factors** of the insight of a single conscious moment, characterized by various essentials.

Clear Vision and Deliverance

13. **"Dependent on seclusion,"** and so on, having the meaning already explained[84] (in the commentary to MN No. 2, that is to say:) "seclusion" is secludedness (from defilement); this is five-fold, namely, seclusion through substitution of opposite qualities, seclusion through suppression (in jhāna), cutting off (by the four paths), tranquillization (by the four fruitions), and renunciation (as Nibbāna). The details should be understood as stated in the commentary to MN No. 1 (Paps I 23f.). Thus as regards the fivefold seclusion, the meaning of "dependent on seclusion" should be understood as "he develops the mindfulness enlightenment factor which is dependent on the seclusion by substitution of opposite qualities,

is dependent on the seclusion by cutting off, is dependent on the seclusion by renunciation." For the yogin who is practising the development of the enlightenment factors accordingly, when he is developing the mindfulness enlightenment factor at the moment of insight, it depends on the seclusion by substitution of opposite qualities as regards function, and on the seclusion by renunciation as regards inclination; but at the moment of the path it depends on the seclusion by cutting off as regards function, and on the seclusion by renunciation as regards object. Some commentators say "it depends on the fivefold seclusion"; for not only do they infer the enlightenment factors in the moments of strong insight, paths, and fruitions, but they also infer them in jhāna produced in a contemplation device which is made the basis for insight, and in jhāna produced in respiration, the foul, and the divine abodes. Nor are they contradicted by the teachers of the commentaries; therefore, in their opinion it is said that at the moment of occurrence of the jhānas it depends on the seclusion by suppression, too, as regards function, and, as in the case of the moment of insight, it depends on the seclusion by renunciation as regards inclination; thus it is correct to say that he develops it depending also on the seclusion of tranquillity.

The same method applies in the case of **"on fading away, on cessation …,"** for these have the same meaning as seclusion. Only that here **"relinquishment"** is twofold; relinquishment as giving up and relinquishment as entering into. Here, "relinquishment as giving up" is the abandoning of the defilements by substitution of opposite qualities at the moment of insight, and by cutting off at the moment of the path; "relinquishment as entering into" is the entering into Nibbāna by inclination thereto at the moment of insight, and by making it the object at the moment of the path. Both these are appropriate in the mixed mundane and supramundane method of commenting; for this mindfulness enlightenment factor thus gives up the defilements and enters into Nibbāna in the way aforesaid.

"Resulting in relinquishment": but this is what is expressed by this phrase as a whole: "changing, changed, and ripening, ripened for the purpose of relinquishment." For this bhikkhu, who is practising the development of the enlightenment factors, develops the mindfulness enlightenment factor according as it is ripening for the purpose of relinquishment as giving up of the defilements, and for the purpose of relinquishment as entering into Nibbāna, and according as it has already ripened. The same method applies to the remaining enlightenment factors.

But here the mindfulness which lays hold of breathing in and out is mundane; mundane breathing in and out perfects the mundane foundations of mindfulness; the mundane foundations of mindfulness perfect the supramundane enlightenment factors; the supramundane enlightenment factors perfect Nibbāna as the fruit of clear vision and deliverance. Thus is the mundane expounded in the place where the mundane has been handed down in the texts, and the supramundane expounded in the place where the supramundane has been handed down in the texts. But the Elder (at the Council) said, "Elsewhere it is thus, but in this sutta, as it is handed down, the supramundane is reached later. Mundane mindfulness of breathing in and out perfects mundane foundations of mindfulness; mundane foundations of mindfulness perfect mundane enlightenment factors; mundane enlightenment factors perfect supramundane Nibbāna as the fruit of clear vision and deliverance. For here, by the term **'clear vision and deliverance'** it is Nibbāna as the fruit of clear vision that is intended."

Part III

THE PAṬISAMBHIDĀ–MAGGA

(Path of Analysis)

Section on Respiration-Mindfulness
(Ānāpānakathā)

Foreword

The first three sections, I to III, are more or less self-evident. Section I is concerned with describing those general states of the mind which hinder and those which help concentration and their various aspects.

Section II deals with particular faulty ways of behaviour of consciousness which hinder progress while practising respiration-mindfulness.

Section III describes how these faults are to be avoided and analyses the process of attaining full concentration, which is treated at some length. It is rounded off with a stanza describing one who has reached arahatship through this practice. The stanza is followed by a commentary which is made the occasion for allusion to Nibbāna—the object of the whole practice—and for a description of the qualities of the Buddha—confidence in whose omniscience provides the impulse to progress until realization by personal experience is attained.

These three sections constitute a kind of general analytical survey and introduction before embarking on the detailed analysis of the actual practice as set forth in the suttas.

Section IV—the main body of the work—at first appears a labyrinth, though examination reveals a systematic and coherent

construction throughout all its length and repetitions. In order to
appreciate this better, one should first of all remember that
respiration-mindfulness is one out of the many methods of developing the four foundations of mindfulness (*cattāro satipaṭṭhānā*)—
"the only way" to attain Nibbāna—and that this development
consists of the constant practice of properly directed mindfulness
and clear comprehension (*sati-sampajañña*). Also, in particular, the
"four tetrads," as they are set out, describe one who is practising
mindfulness *now* ("he knows, 'I breathe in long,'" etc.), and who
is training for *future* attainment as yet unachieved ("'Experiencing
the whole body, I *shall* breathe in,' thus he trains himself," etc.).
Lastly, the order "concentration, insight, path attainment" is
consistently followed and lends architectural unity to the whole.

Bearing these general points in mind, the following construction becomes apparent:

In the first two bases dealing with present knowledge, we have:

(a) analysis of the way the object of contemplation ("Breathing in long," etc.) is known (section 12, pp.67–68);

(b) sections demonstrating how this contemplation is at the
same time the practice of the first foundation of mindfulness (sections 13–14, pp.68–69);

(c) section showing how mindfulness and clear comprehension are simultaneously exercised when concentration has
been obtained and insight applied (section 15, pp.70–
71):

(d) concluding sections listing the states that are present during such concentration, at the successive levels of attainment (sections 16–26, pp.71–74).

In the remaining fourteen bases dealing with training for the
future, the following scheme of construction is adhered to throughout:

   (i)   sections analysing the object of contemplation and its
         treatment ("'Experiencing the whole body, I shall breathe
         in,' thus he trains himself," etc.). This parallels (a) above
         but varies greatly in length and content;

   (ii) sections showing which foundation of mindfulness is
         being practised. This is equal to (b) above;

   (iii) sections dealing with the analysis and description of train-
         ing;

   (iv) sections on mindfulness and clear comprehension (= (c)
         above);

   (v)   concluding sections as in (d) above.

These last four groups are repeated verbatim throughout in each
case, except for the substitution of certain key words where necessary.

In this way each of the sixteen bases is independently brought
up to the point of path attainment.

The last six sections, V to X, merely give a brief classification
of the stages of knowledge, of attainment, of concentration (V),
and insight (VI), and the kinds of knowledge leading up to the
path (VII to IX) and fruition (X). These are dealt with in detail in
the *Visuddhimagga*, Chap. XXI, and in the *Paṭisambhidā Ñāṇakathā*
Sections 5f.; a brief summary is given in Note 95 (see pp.143–44).

The paragraph numbers of the PTS edition are given in brackets
for reference to the text. They are, however, inconsistent in the
later sections and apt to be confusing.

What follows is an attempt to present the contents of the
Ānāpānakathā in a form which, while much compressed for the
purpose of wieldiness, still preserves intact the development,
arrangement, and proportions of the original.

THE ANALYSIS
(§ = paragraph of PTS edition)

Synopsis

1. (§1). For one who develops the sixteen-based[1] respiration-mindfulness[2] concentration, more than two hundred kinds of knowledge arise, namely:

I.	8 kinds of knowledge of obstacles,
	8 kinds of knowledge of aids,
II.	18 kinds of knowledge of imperfections,
III.	13 kinds of knowledge of purification,
IV.	32 kinds of knowledge of exercise of mindfulness,
V.	24 kinds of knowledge through concentration,
VI.	72 kinds of knowledge through insight,
VII.	8 kinds of knowledge of revulsion,
VIII.	8 kinds of knowledge in conformity with revulsion,
IX.	8 kinds of knowledge of tranquillization of revulsion,
X.	21 kinds of knowledge of the bliss of deliverance.

I. The Eight Kinds of Knowledge of Obstacles and the Eight Kinds of Knowledge of Aids

2. (§2).

8 Obstacles to Concentration		8 Aids to Concentration	
(i)	lust,	(i)	renunciation,
(ii)	ill will,	(ii)	non-ill will,
(iii)	stiffness-and-torpor,	(iii)	perception of light,
(iv)	agitation,	(iv)	non-distraction,
(v)	uncertainty,	(v)	defining of states,
(vi)	ignorance,	(vi)	knowledge,
(vii)	aversion,	(vii)	joy,
(viii)	all unprofitable states.	(viii)	all profitable states.

In these sixteen ways the well-composed mind establishes the unities[3] and is purified of the hindrances.[4]

3. (§3). The unities are the above eight aids. The hindrances are the above eight obstacles.

(§4). (i) Renunciation is among the noble ones' outlets (from the defilements), and by that renunciation the noble ones are let out.[5] Lust is an obstruction to the outlet, and through being shut in by that lust one does not understand renunciation as the noble one's outlet.

(ii) to (viii) Same as above for each pair.

But for one whose mind is purified of these hindrances and who develops the sixteen-based respiration-mindfulness concentration, the following eighteen imperfections arise in momentary succession.[6]

II. The Eighteen Kinds of Knowledge of Imperfections

4. (§5). The following are obstacles to concentration:

(i)   The internally distracted consciousness of one who follows with mindfulness the beginning, middle, and end of the in-breath.[7]

(ii) The externally distracted consciousness of one who follows with mindfulness the beginning, middle, and end of the out-breath.[8]

(iii) A state of craving consisting of desire for, and expectation of, in-breath.[9]

(iv) A state of craving consisting of desire for, and expectation of, out-breath.[10]

(v)   Longing for the obtaining of the out-breath by one wearied by the in-breath.[11]

(vi) Longing for the obtaining of the in-breath by one wearied by the out-breath.[12]

The mindfulness that follows out-breath,
And which follows in-breath, too;
Expecting distraction inwardly,
Loving distraction outwardly;
The longing for out-breath in one
Who is by in-breath much oppressed;
The longing for in-breath in one
Who is by out-breath much oppressed:

These six defects of concentration
On respiration-mindfulness
Are those whereby the mind of one
Who is distracted is not freed;
And they who know not liberation
Perforce must trust in others' words.

  (§6).

(vii)   Consciousness which wavers in regard to the in-breath
         when one adverts to the sign.[13]

(viii)   Consciousness which wavers in regard to the sign when
         one adverts to the in-breath.

 (ix)   Consciousness which wavers in regard to the out-breath
         when one adverts to the sign.

  (x)   Consciousness which wavers in regard to the sign when
         one adverts to the out-breath.

 (xi)   Consciousness which wavers in regard to the out-breath
         when one adverts to the in-breath.

(xii)   Consciousness which wavers in regard to the in-breath
         when one adverts to the out-breath.

  Adverting to the sign, his mind
  Distracted is about in-breath;
  Adverting to in-breath, his mind,
  Distracted is about the sign;

Adverting to the sign, his mind
Distracted is about out-breath;
Adverting to out-breath, his mind
Distracted is about the sign;
Adverting to in-breath, his mind
Distracted is about out-breath;
Adverting to out-breath, his mind
Distracted is about in-breath.

These six defects of concentration
On respiration-mindfulness
Are those whereby the mind of one
Who is distracted is not freed;
And they who know not liberation
Perforce must trust in others' words.

(§7).

(xiii)   Consciousness which runs after the past (breaths) and is attacked by distraction.[14]

(xiv)   Consciousness which looks forward to the future (breaths) and is attacked by wavering.[15]

(xv)   Slack consciousness attacked by indolence.

(xvi)   Over-exerted consciousness attacked by agitation.

(xvii)   Consciousness which is attracted and attacked by greed.[16]

(xviii)   Consciousness which is discontented and attacked by ill will.[17]

The consciousness that hunts the past,
That loves the future, that is slack,
Or over-exerted, or attracted,
Or repelled, is not one-pointed.

These six defects of concentration
On respiration-mindfulness
Are those whereby one stained in thought
Knows not the higher consciousness.

(§8). By reason of each of these eighteen imperfections both body and mind are disturbed, unsettled, and unsteady.

> One whose mindfulness of breathing
> Is undeveloped and imperfect,
> Remains unsettled in his body,
> Remains unsettled in his mind,
> Remains unsteady in his body,
> Remains unsteady in his mind.

> One whose mindfulness of breathing
> Is both developed and perfected,
> Remains quite settled in his body,
> Remains quite settled in his mind,
> Remains quite steady in his body,
> Remains quite steady in his mind.

III The Thirteen Kinds of Knowledge of Purification

5. (§9). Consciousness becoming distracted is avoided for the following six reasons:

(i)   By avoiding consciousness which runs after the past (breaths) and is attacked by distraction, (consciousness) is concentrated in one place.[18]

(ii) By avoiding consciousness which looks forward to the future (breaths) and is attacked by wavering, (consciousness) is fixed (there).

(iii) By exerting[19] slack consciousness attacked by indolence, one abandons indolence.

(iv) By restraining[20] over-exerted consciousness attacked by agitation, one abandons agitation.

(v)   By being clearly comprehending[21] about consciousness which is attracted and attacked by greed, one abandons greed.

(vi)   By being clearly comprehending[22] about consciousness which is discontented and attacked by ill will, one abandons ill will.

For these six reasons consciousness becomes purified, cleansed, and arrives at the unities. These are:

(§10).

(vii)   The unity which is the establishing of relinquishment in giving[23] which is (peculiar) to those resolved on generosity.

(viii)   The unity which is the establishment of the sign of tranquillity which is (peculiar) to those who practise the higher consciousness.[24]

(ix)   The unity which is the establishment of the characteristic of decay which is (peculiar) to those who have insight.[25]

(x)   The unity which is the establishment of cessation which is (peculiar) to the noble persons.[26]

Consciousness having become one-pointed for these four reasons is then:

(xi)   entered into purity of practice,[27]

(xii)   grown strong in equanimity,[28]

(xiii)   gladdened by knowledge.[29]

The Beginning, Middle, and End of Contemplation

6. (§11). Purity of practice is the beginning, strengthening in equanimity is the middle, and gladdening the end, of the following:

the four fine-material jhānas,[30]
the four immaterial jhānas,[31]
the eighteen principal insights,[32]
the four paths.[33]

(§12). There are three characteristics of purity of practice as the beginning:

(a)   The mind is purified of its obstructions.

(b)   Through purification the mind arrives at the central (state of equipoise which is the) sign of tranquillity.[34]

(c)   Because of having arrived at that, consciousness enters into (that state).

Hence, these states are called good in the beginning and endowed with characteristics.

(§13). There are three characteristics of strengthening in equanimity as the middle:

(d)   The purified mind looks on with equanimity.[35]

(e)   Being arrived at tranquillity, it looks on with equanimity.

(f)   Having established the unities, it looks on with equanimity.

Hence, these states are called good in the middle and endowed with characteristics.

(§14). There are four characteristics of gladdening as the end:

(g)   Gladdening on account of the non-excess of any of the mental states arisen therein.[36]

(h)   Gladdening on account of the single nature of the faculties.

(i)   Gladdening on account of the sustaining power of the energy which is in conformity therewith.

(j)   Gladdening through cultivation.

Hence, these states are called good in the end and endowed with characteristics.

7. (§§11–20). The consciousness which has thus attained the threefold course (xi, xii, and xiii above), and is good in the three

ways, and is possessed of the characteristics (a–j), is possessed of mental resolution and of the five faculties.

In addition, in the first fine-material jhāna, it is possessed of (the jhāna factors of) applied thought, sustained thought, rapture, and bliss; and likewise, in the eighteen principal insights and the four paths. In the second fine-material jhāna, it is possessed of rapture and bliss. In the third fine-material jhāna, it is possessed of bliss. In the fourth fine-material jhāna, and in the four immaterial jhānas, it is possessed of equanimity.

The Simile of the Saw

8. (§21).

> Sign, in-breath, out-breath, are not object
> Of a single consciousness;
> By one who knows not these three things,
> Development is not obtained.

> Sign, in-breath, out-breath, are not object
> Of a single consciousness;
> By one who does know these three things,
> Development will be obtained.

(§22). It is as though a man were to cut with a saw a tree trunk placed on level ground. His mindfulness is established by the teeth of the saw at the point where they come into contact with the tree trunk, without his giving attention to the teeth of the saw as they approach and recede, although he is not unaware of these; and he manifests endeavour, accomplishes the task, and achieves distinction.

As the tree trunk on the level ground, so the sign for the binding (of mindfulness).[37] As the teeth of the saw, so the in- and out-breaths. As the man's mindfulness is established by the teeth of the saw at the point where they come into contact with the tree trunk, without his giving attention to the teeth of the saw as they approach and recede, although he is not unaware of these, so he manifests endeavour, accomplishes the task, and achieves distinction—so, indeed, the bhikkhu sits, having established his mindfulness at the nose-tip or on the upper lip, without giving attention to the in- and out-breaths as they approach and recede, although he is not unaware of these, and he manifests endeavour, accomplishes the task, and achieves distinction.

(§23). The body and the mind of one who is energetic become pliable—this is the endeavour. The imperfections of one who is energetic are abandoned and his applied thinking is pacified—this is the task. The fetters of one who is energetic are abandoned and his inherent tendencies are brought to an end—this is the distinction.

The Perfecting of Respiration-mindfulness

9. (§24).

> Whose mindfulness of breathing in
> And out is perfect, well developed,
> Gradually brought to growth
> According as the Buddha taught,
> 'Tis he who illuminates the world,
> Like the full moon freed from cloud.[38]

Commentary on the Foregoing Stanza

10. "Breathing in" is the in-breath, not the out-breath; "out" is the out-breath, not the in-breath. The establishment (foundation) by way of the in-breath is mindfulness; the establishment (foundation) by way of the out-breath is mindfulness. It is established (founded) for him who breathes in; it is established (founded) for him who breathes out.[39]

"Perfect": it is made perfect in the sense of laying hold (with mindfulness), in the sense of converging (of the mental faculties), in the sense of perfecting.[40]

"Well-developed": there are four kinds of development, namely:

(i)   on account of the non-excess of any of the mental
        states arisen therein;

(ii)   on account of the single nature of the faculties;

(iii)   on account of the sustaining power of the energy
        which is in conformity therewith;

(iv)   on account of cultivation.

For him these four kinds of development are:

(a)   made the vehicle,

(b)   made the basis,

(c)   practised,

(d)   increased,

(e)   well undertaken.

(§25).

(a)   "Made the vehicle": whenever he wishes, therein he has
      mastery, has power, has perfect confidence; these states
      are bound up with his adverting, wishing, paying atten-
      tion, mind, thinking.

(b)   "Made the basis": on whatever basis[41] the mind is fixed,
      on that mindfulness is well established (founded); on
      whatever basis mindfulness is well-established (founded),
      on that the mind is fixed.

(c)   "Practised": wherever the mind is directed, there mind-
      fulness is diverted to; wherever mindfulness is diverted
      to, there the mind is directed.

(d)   "Increased": increased through laying hold, through con-
      verging, through perfecting. One who lays hold with
      mindfulness conquers evil, unprofitable states.

(e)   "Well undertaken": there are four ways of being well
      undertaken:

    (i)   on account of the non-excess of any of the mental states arisen therein;

    (ii)   on account of the single nature of the faculties;

    (iii) on account of the sustaining power of the energy which is in conformity therewith;

    (iv) because of the complete abolition of the defilements opposed thereto.

[Note: What follows is a play on the word *susamāradhaṃ* "well undertaken," which is here analysed as *samaṃ* "calm," and *susamaṃ* "absolute calm," and *āraddhaṃ* "undertaken."]

"Calm" is those states that are blameless, profitable, and partake of enlightenment—these are "calm." "Absolute calm" is the object of any such states, which is cessation, Nibbāna—this is "absolute calm." So this "calm" and this "absolute calm" are known, seen, experienced, realized, attained, through understanding; tireless energy is "undertaken," unremitting mindfulness is established (founded), the untroubled body is tranquillized, the concentrated mind is one-pointed.

(§26). "Gradually brought to growth": by means of all the sixteen bases of respiration-mindfulness there is successive previous growth and successive subsequent further growth. And all the sixteen-based kinds of respiration-mindfulness are interdependently brought to growth and further growth.

(§27). "According as": there are ten meanings of "according as," namely, those of—

> self-taming,[42]
> self-tranquillizing,
> self-extinction,
> direct knowledge,
> full-understanding,
> abandoning,
> development,

realization,
complete comprehension of the truths,
establishment of cessation.

(§28). "The Buddha": He who is the Blessed One, self-become, having no teacher in things formerly unknown, who himself discovered the Truths, attained to omniscience therein and to mastery of the powers.

"The Buddha": in what sense "the Buddha" (the Enlightened One)? Enlightened because he is the discoverer of the truths, the enlightener of the generation; because of omniscience, of seeing all, of not being enlightened by another, of majesty; through being called one whose cankers are destroyed, through being called freed from the substrata of existence; because he is quite without greed, quite without hate, quite without delusion, quite without defilement, gone by the one path, the only discoverer of the peerless full enlightenment, the destroyer of non-enlightenment, the receiver of enlightenment.

"The Buddha": This is not a name given by a mother nor a father, nor a brother, nor a sister, nor by friends and companions, nor by kindred and relatives, nor by recluses and brahmans, nor by deities. It is the name for the ultimate liberation of enlightenment of the Blessed One, together with the omniscient knowledge received at the root of the Tree of Wisdom; it is a designation based on realization, that is to say, this name "the Buddha."

(§29). "Taught": taught by the Buddha in the ten meanings of "according as" (see above).

"He" is a layman or one gone forth.

"World": the world of the aggregates, of the elements, of the sense bases, the world of misfortune, the world of the origin of misfortune, the world of good fortune, the world of the origin of good fortune.

| One world | : | all beings are maintained by nutriment. |
| Two worlds | : | mentality and materiality. |

Three worlds	:	three feelings.[43]
Four worlds	:	four nutriments.[44]
Five worlds	:	five aggregates (as objects) of clinging.[45]
Six worlds	:	six internal sense bases.[46]
Seven worlds	:	seven stations of consciousness.[47]
Eight worlds	:	eight worldly conditions.[48]
Nine worlds	:	nine abodes of beings.[49]
Ten worlds	:	ten sense bases.[50]
Twelve worlds	:	twelve sense bases.[51]
Eighteen worlds	:	eighteen elements.[52]

(§30). "Illuminates": because of being enlightened in the ten meanings of "according as" he lights up, illumines, illuminates this world.

(§31). "Like the full moon freed from cloud": as the clouds, so are the defilements; like the moon so is the noble ones' knowledge; like the full moon, the deity, so is the bhikkhu; as the moon freed from cloud, freed from mist, freed from smoke and dust, freed from the clutches of Rāhu,[53] shines and glows and radiates, so, indeed, the bhikkhu freed from all defilements, shines and glows and radiates.

IV. The Thirty-two kinds of Knowledge of Exercise of Mindfulness

Statement of the Method

11. (§32). (This consists of a repetition of the four tetrads as set forth in the sutta beginning with **"Here, … a bhikkhu, gone to the forest …"** and ending with **"'… contemplating relinquishment, I shall breathe out,' thus he trains himself"**—see pp.5-7).

Analysis of the Method

(§33). **"Here"**: in this view, in this experience, in this choice, in this belief, in this norm, in this discipline, in this norm and discipline, in this word, in this life of purity, in this Master's Dispensation.

"**A bhikkhu**": a noble commoner, or a trainer, or an unshakable arahat.[54]

"**Forest**": having gone out beyond the boundary post, all that is forest.

"**Root of a tree**": where the bhikkhu's seat, or stool, or cushion, or mat, or piece of hide, or spread of grass, or leaves, or pile of straw, is prepared—there he walks, stands, sits, or lies down.

"**Empty**": unfrequented by laymen or by those gone forth.

"**Place**": dwelling, half-gabled building, palace, mansion, cave.[55]

"**Sits down; having folded his legs crosswise**": is seated, having folded his legs crosswise.

"**Set his body erect**": the body is placed well set, erect.

"**Established mindfulness in front of him**": [lit.: "having established (*upaṭṭhapetvā*) mindfulness (*sati*) around (*pari*) the face (*mukhaṃ*)"] "in (*pari*)" in the sense of laying hold (*pariggaha*); "front (*mukhaṃ*)" in the sense of outlet (or leading forth, *niyyāna*); "mindfulness (*sati*)" in the sense of establishing (foundation, *upaṭṭhāna*).[56]

(§34). "**Ever mindful he breathes in, mindful he breathes out**": he is one who practises mindfulness in the thirty-two ways stated above (i.e. the four tetrads, times the two breaths in each case.) For one who knows one-pointedness and non-distraction of mind by means of each of these thirty-two ways, mindfulness is established (founded); by means of that mindfulness and that knowledge, he is one who practises mindfulness.

FIRST TETRAD

12. (§35). "**Breathing in long, he knows, 'I breathe in long'; breathing out long, he knows, 'I breathe out long.'**"

The Nine Ways of Knowing

(a) He breathes in a long in-breath reckoned as a long extent.[57]

(b)   He breathes out a long out-breath reckoned as a long extent.

(c)   He breathes in and breathes out long in-breaths and out-breaths reckoned as a long extent.[58] As he breathes in and breathes out long in-breaths and out-breaths reckoned as a long extent, zeal arises.[59]

(d)   Through zeal he breathes in a long in-breath more subtle than before, reckoned as a long extent.

(e)   Through zeal he breathes out a long out-breath more subtle than before, reckoned as a long extent.

(f)   Through zeal he breathes in and breathes out long in-breaths and out-breaths more subtle than before, reckoned as a long extent. As, through zeal, he breathes in and breathes out long in-breaths and out-breaths more subtle than before reckoned as a long extent, joy arises.[60]

(g)   Through joy he breathes in a long in-breath more subtle than before, reckoned as a long extent.

(h)   Through joy he breathes out a long out-breath more subtle than before, reckoned as a long extent.

(i)   Through joy he breathes in and breathes out long in-breaths and out-breaths more subtle than before, reckoned as a long extent. As, through joy, he breathes in and breathes out long in-breaths and out-breaths more subtle than before reckoned as a long extent, the mind turns away from the long in-breaths and out-breaths,[61] and equanimity is established.[62]

The Foundation of Mindfulness

13. In these nine ways *long in-breaths and out-breaths* are the *body.*[63]

The establishment (foundation) is mindfulness.[64]

Contemplation is knowledge.[65]

The *body* is the establishment (foundation), but it is not mindfulness.[66]

Mindfulness is both the establishment (foundation) and mindfulness.[67]

By means of that mindfulness and that knowledge he contemplates that *body*.[68]

Hence it is called, "The development of the establishment (foundation) of mindfulness consisting of contemplation of the *body in the body*."[69]

14. (§36). "He contemplates that *body*," means:

He contemplates as impermanent, not as permanent; and in doing so, he abandons the perception of permanence.

He contemplates as suffering, not as pleasure; and in doing so, he abandons the perception of pleasure.

He contemplates as non-self, not as self; and in doing so, he abandons the perception of self.

He feels revulsion, does not enjoy; and in doing so, he abandons enjoying.

He becomes dispassionate, without greed; and in doing so, he abandons greed.

He causes cessation, not arising; and in doing so, he abandons arising.

He renounces, does not cling; and in doing so, he abandons clinging.

"Development": there are four kinds of development:

   (i)   on account of non-excess of any of the mental states arisen therein;

   (ii)   on account of the single nature of the faculties;

   (iii) on account of the sustaining power of the energy which is in conformity therewith;

   (iv)   on account of cultivation.

Mindfulness and Clear Comprehension

15. (§37). For one who knows one-pointedness and non-distraction of mind by means of *long in-breaths and out-breaths*, feelings
are known as they arise, known as they appear, known as they
subside. Perceptions are known as they arise, known as they appear, known as they subside. Applied thoughts are known as they
arise, known as they appear, known as they subside.

(§38). With the arising of ignorance there is the arising of feeling; with the arising of craving there is the arising of feeling; with
the arising of kamma there is the arising of feeling; with the arising of sense-impression[71] there is the arising of feeling. Thus the
arising of feeling is known in the sense of arising through the arising of conditions. For one who sees the characteristics of being
produced, the arising of feeling is known.

To one who brings them to mind as impermanent,[72] the appearance of dissolution is known. To one who brings them to mind as
suffering, the appearance of fear is known. To one who brings
them to mind as non-self, the appearance of voidness is known.

With the cessation of ignorance there is the cessation of feeling;
with the cessation of craving there is the cessation of feeling; with
the cessation of kamma there is the cessation of feeling; with the
cessation of sense-impression there is the cessation of feeling. Thus
the cessation of feeling is known in the sense of ceasing through
the ceasing of conditions. For one who sees the characteristic of
change, the cessation of feeling is known.

(§39). With the arising of ignorance there is the arising of perception ...

To one who brings them to mind as impermanent, the appearance of dissolution is known ...

With the cessation of ignorance there is the cessation of perception ...

(§40). With the arising of ignorance there is the arising of applied thoughts; with the arising of craving there is the arising of

applied thoughts; with the arising of kamma there is the arising of applied thoughts; with the arising of perception[73] there is the arising of applied thoughts. Thus the arising of applied thoughts is known in the sense of arising through the arising of conditions. For one who sees the characteristics of being produced, the arising of applied thoughts is known.

To one who brings them to mind as impermanent, the appearance of dissolution is known ...

With the cessation of ignorance there is the cessation of applied thoughts ...

The Bringing to Bear of the Faculties, etc.

16. (§41). One who knows one-pointedness and non-distraction of mind by means of *long in-breaths and out-breaths*, brings to bear[74] the faculties, the powers, the enlightenment factors, the path, mental objects, knows the domain, penetrates the meaning of calm.

17. "Brings to bear the faculties": he brings to bear—
the faith faculty in the sense of resolve;
the energy faculty in the sense of exertion;
the mindfulness faculty in the sense of establishment (foundation);
the concentration faculty in the sense of non-distraction;
the understanding faculty in the sense of seeing.

This person brings to bear these faculties on this object.

18. "Knows the domain": that which is his object is his domain; that which is his domain is his object; the person understands through understanding.

"Calm": the establishment of the object is calm; non-distraction of mind is calm; resolution of mind is calm; purification of mind is calm.

"Meaning" is the blameless meaning, undefiled meaning, purified meaning, highest meaning.

"Penetrates": he penetrates the establishment (foundation) of the object, the sense of non-distraction of mind, the sense of resolution of mind, the sense of purification of mind.

19. (§42). "Brings to bear the powers": he brings to bear—

	in the sense of non-wavering in (the face of)	
the faith power		faithlessness;
the energy power	"	indolence;
the mindfulness power	"	negligence;
the concentration power	"	agitation;
the understanding power	"	ignorance.

This person brings to bear these powers on this object.

20. "Knows the domain," etc. (as in 18 above).

21. (§43). "Brings to bear the enlightenment factors": he brings to bear—

the mindfulness enlightenment factor in the sense of establishing (foundation);

the investigation-of-states e.f.	"		enquiry;
the energy e.f.	"	"	exertion;
the rapture e.f.	"	"	pervasion;
the tranquillity e.f.	"	"	calmness;
the concentration e.f.	"	"	non-distraction;
the equanimity e.f.	"	"	reflection.

This person brings to bear these enlightenment factors on this object.

22. "Knows the domain," etc. (as in 18 above).

23. (§ 44). "Brings to bear the path": he brings to bear—

right understanding	in the sense of seeing;
right thinking	in the sense of focusing;
right speech	in the sense of laying hold;
right action	in the sense of originating;

right livelihood	in the sense of purifying;
right effort	in the sense of exertion;
right mindfulness	in the sense of establishment (foundation);
right concentration	in the sense of non-distraction.

This person brings to bear this path on this object.

24. "Knows the domain," etc. (as in 18 above).

25. (§45). "Brings to bear mental objects": he brings to bear[74]—

the faculties	in the sense of predominance;
the powers	in the sense of non-wavering;
the enlightenment factors	in the sense of outlet;
the path	in the sense of cause;
the foundation of mindfulness	in the sense of establishment (foundation)
right effort	in the sense of striving;
the road to power	in the sense of success;
truth	in the sense of reality;
tranquillity	in the sense of non-distraction;
insight	in the sense of contemplation;
tranquillity and insight	in the sense of single nature,
yoking (of the above two)	in the sense of non-excess (of either);
purity of conduct	in the sense of restraint;
purity of mind	in the sense of non-distraction;
purity of view	in the sense of seeing;
liberation	in the sense of deliverance;
clear vision	in the sense of penetration;
deliverance	in the sense of giving up;

knowledge of destruction	in the sense of cutting off;
knowledge of non-arising	in the sense of tranquillization;
zeal	in the sense of root cause;
bringing-to-mind	in the sense of arousing;
impression	in the sense of bringing to bear;
feeling	in the sense of meeting together;
concentration	in the sense of being foremost;
mindfulness	in the sense of predominance;
understanding	in the sense of surpassing;
deliverance	in the sense of essence;
deathless Nibbāna	in the sense of end.

This person brings to bear these mental objects on this object.

26. "Knows the domain," etc. (as in 18 above).

27. (§46) **"Breathing in short, he knows, 'I breathe in short'; breathing out short, he knows, 'I breathe out short.'"**

The Nine Ways of Knowing

(a) He breathes in a short in-breath which takes a brief time (and so on as in 12 (b) to (i) substituting "short" for "long").

The Foundation of Mindfulness

28. In these nine ways *short in-breaths and out-breaths* are the *body*.

The establishment (foundation) is mindfulness.

Contemplation is knowledge.

The *body* is the establishment (foundation) but it is not mindfulness.

Mindfulness is both the establishment (foundation) and mindfulness.

By means of that mindfulness and that knowledge he contemplates that *body*.

Hence it is called, "The development of the establishment (foundation) of mindfulness consisting of contemplation of the *body in the body*."

29. (§47). "He contemplates that body," etc. (as in 14 above).

Mindfulness and Clear Comprehension

30. For one who knows one-pointedness and non-distraction of mind by means of *short in-breaths and out-breaths*, feelings are known as they arise, etc. (as in 15 above).

The Bringing to Bear of the Faculties, etc.

31–41. One who knows one-pointedness and non-distraction of mind by means of *short in-breaths and out-breaths*, brings to bear the faculties ..., etc. (as in 16–26 above).

42. (§48). **"'Experiencing the whole body,' I shall breathe in, thus he trains himself; 'experiencing the whole body,' I shall breathe out, thus he trains himself."**

"Body": There are two bodies—the mentality-body and the materiality-body.

Feeling, perception, volition, sense-impression, attention—mentality and the mentality-body—and those (things) which are called the mental formations—this is the mentality-body.[76]

The four great primaries and the materiality derived from the four great primaries —in-breath and out-breath and the sign for the binding (of mindfulness)—and those (things) which are called the bodily formations—this is the materiality-body.[77]

43. (§49). "Experiencing": for one who knows one-pointedness and non-distraction of mind through *breathing in long, breathing out long, breathing in short, breathing out short*, mindfulness is

established. By means of that mindfulness and that knowledge those *bodies* are experienced.[78] They are experienced by one—

> who adverts,
> who knows,
> who sees,
> who reflects,
> who mentally decides,
> who resolves with faith,
> who exerts energy,
> who establishes mindfulness,
> who concentrates the mind,
> who understands through understanding,
> who directly knows what should be directly known,
> who fully understands what should be fully understood,
> who abandons what should be abandoned,
> who develops what should be developed,
> who realizes what should be realized.

The Foundation of Mindfulness

44. *Breathing in and out experiencing the whole body* are the *body.*

The establishment (foundation) is mindfulness.

Contemplation is knowledge.

The *body* is the establishment (foundation), but it is not mindfulness.

Mindfulness is both the establishment (foundation) and mindfulness.

By means of that mindfulness and that knowledge he contemplates that *body.*

Hence it is called "The development of the establishment (foundation) of mindfulness consisting of contemplation of the *body in the body.*"

45. (§50). "He contemplates that *body,*" etc. (as in 14 above).

The Three Higher Trainings

46. *Breathing in and out experiencing the whole body* is purity of conduct in the sense of restraint, purity of consciousness in the sense of non-distraction, and purity of view in the sense of seeing.[79]

What is restraint therein is the training in the higher virtuous conduct; what is non-distraction therein is the training in the higher consciousness; what is seeing therein is the training in the higher understanding. He trains himself in these three trainings:

by adverting,

by knowing,

... (and so on as in 43 above) ...

by realizing what should be realized.

Mindfulness and Clear Comprehension

47. For one who knows one-pointedness and non-distraction of mind by means of *breathing in and out experiencing the whole body*, feelings are known as they arise, etc. (as in 15 above).

The Bringing to Bear of the Faculties, etc.

48–58. One who knows one-pointedness and non-distraction of mind by means of *breathing in and out experiencing the whole body,* brings to bear the faculties, etc. (as in 16–26 above).

59. (§51). **"'Calming the bodily formation, I shall breathe in,' thus he trains himself; 'calming the bodily formation, I shall breathe out,' thus he trains himself."**

"Bodily-formation": *long in-breaths, long out-breaths, short in-breaths, short out-breaths, breathing in experiencing the whole body, breathing out experiencing the whole body*—these things are bodily properties; being bound up with the body they are *bodily formations.*[80] He trains himself by **calming,** causing to cease, pacifying, those bodily formations.

Such bodily formations whereby there is bending backward, sideways, all ways, forward, shaking, trembling, moving of the body—

"'calming the bodily formation, I shall breathe in,' thus he trains himself; 'calming the bodily formation, I shall breathe out,' thus he trains himself."

Such bodily formations whereby there is no bending backward, sideways, all ways, forward, shaking, trembling, moving of the body—"'Calming the quiet and subtle bodily formation, I shall breathe in,' thus he trains himself; 'calming the quiet and subtle bodily formation, I shall breathe out,' thus he trains himself."

The Simile of the Gong

60. (If) it is thus, (it is objected): "'Calming the bodily formation, I shall breathe in,' thus he trains himself; 'calming the bodily formation, I shall breathe out,' thus he trains himself'—this being so, there is no production of awareness of wind, and there is no production of the in-and-out breathing, and there is no production of respiration-mindfulness, and there is no production of respiration-mindfulness concentration, and accordingly the wise neither enter into, nor emerge from, that attainment."

(Yet since) it is thus, (it is replied): "'Calming the bodily formation, I shall breathe in,' thus he trains himself; 'calming the bodily formation, I shall breathe out,' thus he trains himself'—this being so, *there is* production of awareness of wind,[81] and *there is* production of the in-and-out breathing, and *there is* production of respiration-mindfulness, and *there is* production of respiration-mindfulness concentration, and accordingly the wise do enter into, and emerge from, that attainment."

Like what? Just as when a metal gong is struck; at first gross sounds occur, and (consciousness proceeds) because the sign[82] of the gross sounds is well grasped, well brought to mind, well considered; and when the gross sounds have ceased, then afterwards faint sounds occur, and (consciousness proceeds) because the sign of the faint sounds is well grasped, well brought to mind, well considered; and when the faint sounds have ceased, then afterwards consciousness proceeds because of having the sign of the faint sounds as object: so indeed, at first gross in-breaths and out-breaths occur and (consciousness does not become distracted) because the sign of the gross in-breaths and out-breaths is well grasped, well brought to mind, well considered; and when the gross in-breaths and out-breaths have ceased, then afterwards faint in-breaths and out-breaths occur, and (consciousness does not become distracted) because the sign of the faint in-breaths and out-breaths is well grasped, well brought to mind, well considered; and when the faint in- and out-breaths have ceased, then afterwards consciousness does not become distracted because of having the sign of the faint in- and out-breaths as object.

This being so, *there is* production of awareness of wind, and *there is* production of the in-and out breathing, and *there is* production of respiration-mindfulness, and *there is* production of respiration-mindfulness concentration, and accordingly the wise do enter into, and emerge from, that attainment.

The Foundation of Mindfulness

61. *Breathing in and out calming the bodily formation is the body.*

The establishment (foundation) is mindfulness.

Contemplation is knowledge.

The *body* is the establishment (foundation), but it is not mindfulness.

Mindfulness is both the establishment (foundation) and mindfulness.

By means of that mindfulness and that knowledge he contemplates that *body*.

Hence it is called, "The development of the establishment (foundation) of mindfulness consisting of contemplation of the *body in the body*."

62. (§52). "He contemplates that *body*," etc. (as in 14 above).

The Three Higher Trainings

63. *Breathing in and out calming the bodily formation* is purity of conduct in the sense of restraint, etc. (as in 46 above).

Mindfulness and Clear Comprehension

64. For one who knows one-pointedness and non-distraction of mind by means of *breathing in and out calming the bodily formation*, feelings are known as they arise, etc. (as in 15 above).

The Bringing to Bear of the Faculties

65–75. One who knows one-pointedness and non-distraction of mind by means of *breathing in and out calming the bodily formation,* brings to bear the faculties, etc. (as in 16–26 above).

Conclusion of the First Tetrad

There are eight kinds of knowledge of contemplation, eight kinds of establishment (foundation) of mindfulness, four bases from the sutta, concerning contemplation of *the body in the body.*

SECOND TETRAD

76. (§53). "'Experiencing rapture, I shall breathe in,' thus he trains himself; 'experiencing rapture, I shall breathe out,' thus he trains himself."

"Rapture": for one who knows one-pointedness and non-distraction of mind through *breathing in and out in each of the eight modes of the first tetrad* the joy of *rapture* arises.

That rapture which is enjoyment, rejoicing, joyousness, gaiety, happiness, felicity, elation, satisfaction of mind—that is rapture.

77. (§54) "Experiencing": for one who knows one-pointedness and non-distraction of mind through *breathing in and out in each of the eight modes of the first tetrad,* mindfulness is established.

By means of that mindfulness and that knowledge that *rapture* is experienced. It is experienced by one—
who adverts,
who knows,
… (and so on, as in 43 above) …
who realizes what should be realized.

The Foundation of Mindfulness

78. By means of *breathing in and out experiencing rapture* there is *feeling*.
The establishment (foundation) is mindfulness.
Contemplation is knowledge.
Feeling is the establishment (foundation), but it is not mindfulness.
Mindfulness is both the establishment (foundation) and mindfulness.
By means of that mindfulness and that knowledge he contemplates that *feeling*.
Hence it is called, "The development of the establishment (foundation) of mindfulness consisting of contemplation of the *feelings in the feelings*."
79. "He contemplates" that *feeling*," etc. (as in 14 above).

The Three Higher Trainings

80. *Breathing in and out experiencing rapture* is purity of conduct in the sense of restraint, etc. (as in 46 above).

Mindfulness and Clear Comprehension

8. For one who knows one-pointedness and non-distraction of mind by means of *breathing in and out experiencing rapture*, feelings are known as they arise, etc. (as in 15 above).

The Bringing to Bear of the Faculties, etc.

82–92. One who knows one-pointedness and non-distraction of mind by means of *breathing in and out experiencing rapture,* brings to bear the faculties, etc. (as in 16–26 above).

93. (§55). "'Experiencing bliss, I shall breathe in,' thus he trains himself; 'experiencing bliss, I shall breathe out,' thus he trains himself."

"Bliss": there are two kinds of bliss, bodily bliss and mental bliss.[84]

That bodily agreeableness and bodily bliss which is agreeable and blissful experience born of bodily impression, agreeable and blissful feeling born of bodily impression—that is bodily bliss.[85]

That mental agreeableness and mental bliss which is agreeable and blissful experience born of mental impression, agreeable and blissful feeling born of mental impression, that is mental bliss.

94. "Experiencing": For one who knows one-pointedness and non-distraction of mind through *breathing in and out in each of the eight modes of the first tetrad and the first two modes of the second tetrad,* mindfulness is established. By means of that mindfulness and that knowledge that *bliss* is experienced. It is experienced by one—

who adverts,

who knows,

… (and so on, as in 43 above) …

who realizes what should be realized.

The Foundation of Mindfulness

95. By means of *breathing in and out experiencing bliss there is feeling* etc. (as in 78 above).

96–109. (As in 79–92 above, substituting "bliss" for "rapture".)

110. (§56). "'Experiencing the mental formation, I shall breathe in,' thus he trains himself; 'experiencing the mental formation, I shall breathe out,' thus he trains himself."

"**Mental formation**": perception and feeling through *breathing in and out in each of the eight modes of the the first tetrad and the first four modes of the second tetrad*—these things are mental properties, being bound up with the mind, they are mental formations—this is the mental formation.

111. "**Experiencing**": For one who knows one-pointedness and non-distraction of mind through *breathing in and out in each of the eight modes of the first tetrad and the first four modes of the second tetrad,* mindfulness is established. By means of that mindfulness and that knowledge that mental formation is experienced. It is experienced by one—

who adverts,

who knows,

... (and so on, as in 43 above) ...

who realizes what should be realized.

The Foundation of Mindfulness

112. By means of *breathing in and out experiencing the mental formation* there is *feeling,* etc. (as in 78 above).

113–126. (As in 79–92 above, substituting *"the mental formation" for "rapture."*)

127. (§57). "'**Calming the mental formation, I shall breathe in,' thus he trains himself; 'calming the mental formation, I shall breathe out,' thus he trains himself.**"

"**Mental formation**": perception and feeling through *breathing in and out in each of the eight modes of the the first tetrad and the first six modes of the second tetrad*—these things are mental properties, being bound up with the mind they are mental formations—he trains himself by **calming**, causing to cease, pacifying those mental formations.

The Foundation of Mindfulness

128. By means of *breathing in and out calming the mental formation* there is *feeling,* etc. (as in 78 above).

129–142. (As in 79–92 above, substituting *"calming the mental formation"* for *"experiencing rapture."*)

Conclusion of the Second Tetrad

There are eight kinds of knowledge of contemplation, eight kinds of establishment (foundation) of mindfulness, four bases from the sutta, concerning contemplation of *the feelings in the feelings.*

THIRD TETRAD

143. (§58). **"'Experiencing the mind, I shall breathe in,' thus he trains himself; 'experiencing the mind, I shall breathe out,' thus he trains himself."**

"Mind": Through *breathing in and out in each of the eight modes of each of the first two tetrads there is mind which is consciousness;* that mind which is intellect, intellection, heart, lucidity, mind, mind-base, mind-faculty, consciousness, consciousness aggregate, appropriate mind-consciousness element—that is *mind.*[86]

144. **"Experiencing"**: for one who knows one-pointedness and non-distraction of mind through *breathing in and out in each of the eight modes of each of the first two tetrads,* mindfulness is established. By means of that mindfulness and that knowledge that *mind* is experienced. It is experienced by one—

who adverts,

who knows,

… (and so on, as in 43 above) …

who realizes what should be realized.

The Foundation of Mindfulness

145. By means of *breathing in and out experiencing the mind* there is *mind which is consciousness.*

The establishment (foundation) is mindfulness.

Contemplation is knowledge.

Mind which is consciousness is the establishment (foundation), but it is not mindfulness.

Mindfulness is both the establishment (foundation) and mindfulness.

By means of that mindfulness and that knowledge he contemplates that *mind which is consciousness.*

Hence it is called, "The development of the establishment (foundation) of mindfulness consisting of contemplation of the *mind in the mind."*

146. "He contemplates that *mind,"* etc. (as in 14 above).

The Three Higher Trainings

147. *Breathing in and out experiencing the mind* is purity of conduct in the sense of restraint, etc. (as in 46 above).

Mindfulness and Clear Comprehension

148. For one who knows one-pointedness and non-distraction of mind by means of *breathing in and out experiencing the mind,* feelings are known as they arise, etc. (as in 15 above).

The Bringing to Bear of the Faculties, etc.

149–159. One who knows one-pointedness and non-distraction of mind by means of *breathing in and out experiencing the mind,* brings to bear the faculties, etc. (as in 16–26 above).

160. (§59). " 'Gladdening the mind, I shall breathe in,' thus he trains himself; 'gladdening the mind, I shall breathe out,' thus he trains himself."

"**Gladdening**":   For one who knows one-pointedness and non-distraction of mind through *breathing in and out in each of the eight modes of each of the first two tetrads and the first two modes of the third tetrad*, there arises gladdening of the mind. That mental enjoyment which is rejoicing, joyousness, gaiety, happiness, felicity, elation, satisfaction of mind—that is gladdening of the mind.[87]

The Foundation of Mindfulness

161. By means of *breathing in and out gladdening the mind* there is *mind which is consciousness,* etc. (as in 145 above).

162–175. (As in 146–159 above, substituting "*gladdening*" for "*experiencing.*")

176. (§60). "'**Concentrating the mind, I shall breathe in,**' thus he trains himself; 'concentrating the mind, I shall breathe out,' thus he trains himself.**"

"**Concentrating**":   one-pointedness and non-distraction of mind through *breathing in and out in each of the eight modes of each of the first two tetrads and the first six modes of the third tetrad is* concentration; that establishment, stability, steadiness, which is undisturbedness, non-distraction, undisturbed intellection, tranquillity, concentration faculty, concentration power, right concentration—that is concentration.[88]

The Foundation of Mindfulness

177. By means of *breathing in and out concentrating the mind* there is *mind which is consciousness,* etc. (as in 145 above).

178–191. (As in 146–159 above, substituting "*concentrating*" for "*experiencing.*")

192. (§51). "'**Liberating the mind, I shall breathe in,**' thus he trains himself; 'liberating the mind, I shall breathe out,' thus he trains himself.**"

"'Liberating the mind from greed, I shall breathe in,' thus he trains himself; 'liberating the mind from greed, I shall breathe out,' thus he trains himself."

Similarly with hate, delusion, pride, wrong view, uncertainty, stiffness-and-torpor, agitation, lack of shame, lack of moral dread.

The Foundation of Mindfulness

193. By means of breathing *in and out liberating the mind* there is *mind which is consciousness,* etc. (as in 145 above).

194–207. (As in 146–159 above, substituting *"liberating"* for *"experiencing."*)

Conclusion of the Third Tetrad

There are eight kinds of knowledge of contemplation, eight kinds of establishment (foundation) of mindfulness, four bases from the sutta, concerning contemplation of *the mind in the mind.*

Fourth Tetrad

208. (§62). **"'Contemplating impermanence, I shall breathe in,' thus he trains himself; 'contemplating impermanence, I shall breathe out,' thus he trains himself."**

"Impermanence": The five aggregates are impermanent in the sense of rise and fall.[89] One who sees the rise of the five aggregates sees twenty-five characteristics.[90] One who sees the fall of the five aggregates sees twenty-five characteristics. One who sees the rise and fall of the five aggregates sees fifty characteristics.

209. Contemplating impermanence in materiality, I shall breathe in, thus he trains himself; contemplating impermanence in materiality, I shall breathe out, thus he trains himself."

"Contemplating impermanence in feeling … trains himself.

"Contemplating impermanence in perception … trains himself.

"Contemplating impermanence in formations … trains himself.

"Contemplating impermanence in consciousness … trains himself.

(And similarly in respect of each single thing in the following groups:)[91]

the six internal sense-bases,
the six external sense-bases,
the sixfold consciousness group,
the sixfold sense-impression group,
the sixfold feeling group,
the sixfold perception group,
the sixfold volition group,
the sixfold craving group,
the sixfold applied thought group,
the sixfold sustained thought group,
the six elements (beginning with earth),
the ten kasiṇas (ending with consciousness),
the thirty-two parts of the body,
the twelve internal and external sense-bases,
the eighteen elements,
the twenty-two faculties,
the three elements (beginning with sense-desire),
the nine kinds of existence,
the four fine-material jhānas,
the four mind deliverances,
the four immaterial jhānas,
the twelve links of dependent origination.

The Foundation of Mindfulness

210. By means of *breathing in and out contemplating imperma-nence* there are *mental objects*.

The establishment (foundation) is mindfulness.

Contemplation is knowledge.

Mental objects are the establishment (foundation), but they are not mindfulness.

Mindfulness is both the establishment (foundation) and mind-fulness.

By means of that mindfulness and that knowledge he contem-plates those *mental objects*.

Hence it is called, "The development of the establishment (foundation) of mindfulness consisting of contemplation of mental objects in *mental objects*."

211. "He contemplates those *mental objects*," etc. (as in 14 above).

The Three Higher Trainings

212. *Breathing in and out contemplating impermanence* is purity of conduct in the sense of restraint, etc. (as in 46 above).

Mindfulness and Clear Comprehension

213. For one who knows one-pointedness and non-distraction of mind by means of *breathing in and out contemplating impermanence*, feelings are known as they arise, etc. (as in 15 above).

The Bringing to Bear of the Faculties, etc.

214–224. One who knows one-pointedness and non-distraction of mind by means of *breathing in and out contemplating impermanence*, brings to bear the faculties, etc. (as in 16–26 above).

225. (§63). "'**Contemplating fading away, I shall breathe in,' thus he trains himself; 'contemplating fading away, I shall breathe out,' thus he trains himself.**"

Seeing danger in materiality, he is filled with the desire for the **fading away** of materiality, is resolute in faith, and his mind is firmly decided.[92]

"'Contemplating fading away of materiality, I shall breathe in,' thus he trains himself; 'contemplating fading away of materiality, I shall breathe out,' thus he trains himself."

(Similar paragraphs for each of the items listed in 209.)

The Foundation of Mindfulness

226. By means of *breathing in and out contemplating fading away* there are *mental objects*, etc. (as in 210 above).

227–240. (As in 211–224 above, substituting *'fading away'* for *"impermanence."*)

241. (§64). **"'Contemplating cessation, I shall breathe in,' thus he trains himself; 'contemplating cessation, I shall breathe out,' thus he trains himself."**

Seeing danger in materiality, he is filled with desire for the **cessation** of materiality, is resolute in faith, and his mind is firmly decided.

"'Contemplating cessation of materiality, I shall breathe in,' thus he trains himself; 'contemplating cessation of materiality, I shall breathe out,' thus he trains himself."

(Similar paragraphs for each of the items listed in 209 above.)

242. (§65). There is danger through ignorance in five ways:

> in the sense of impermanence,
> in the sense of suffering,
> in the sense of non-self,
> in the sense of burning,
> in the sense of change.

There is cessation of ignorance in eight ways:

> with the cessation of origination,
> with the cessation of arising,
> with the cessation of birth,
> with the cessation of producing,
> with the cessation of cause,
> with the cessation of condition,
> with the arising of knowledge,
> with the manifestation of cessation.

Seeing danger through ignorance in these five ways, with the cessation of ignorance in these eight ways, he is filled with zeal, resolute in faith, and his mind is firmly decided.

"'Contemplating the cessation of ignorance, I shall breathe in,' thus he trains himself; 'contemplating the cessation of ignorance, I shall breathe out,' thus he trains himself."[93]

(§66) There is danger through formations in five ways: (and so on, with similar paragraphs for each of the remaining ten links of dependent origination, namely: consciousness, mentality-materiality, sixfold sense-base, sense-impression, feeling, craving, clinging, becoming, birth, old-age-and-death).

The Foundation of Mindfulness

243. By means of *breathing in and out contemplating cessation* there are *mental objects,* etc. (as in 210 above).

244–257. (As in 211–224 above, substituting "cessation" for "impermanence.")

258. (§67). "'Contemplating relinquishment, I shall breathe in,' thus he trains himself; 'contemplating relinquishment, I shall breathe out,' thus he trains himself."

"Relinquishment": there are two kinds of relinquishment, relinquishment as giving up and relinquishment as entering into.

Relinquishment as giving up, gives up materiality; the entering of the mind into the cessation of materiality, into Nibbāna, is relinquishment as entering into.

"'Contemplating relinquishment of materiality, I shall breathe in,' thus he trains himself; 'contemplating relinquishment of materiality, I shall breathe out,' thus he trains himself."

Relinquishment as giving up, gives up feelings; (and so on, with similar paragraphs for each of the items listed in 209 above).

The Foundation of Mindfulness

259. By means of *breathing in and out contemplating relinquishment* there are *mental objects,* etc. (as in 210 above).

260–273. (As in 211–224 above, substituting "*relinquishment*" for "*impermanence.*")

Conclusion of the Fourth Tetrad

There are eight kinds of knowledge of contemplation, eight kinds of establishment (foundation) of mindfulness, four bases from the sutta, concerning contemplation of *mental objects in mental objects*.

V. The Twenty-four Kinds of Knowledge through Concentration[95]

274. (§68). These are the one-pointedness and non-distraction of mind by means of breathing in and breathing out in each of the four bases of each of the first three tetrads.

VI. The Seventy-two Kinds of Knowledge through Insight

275. These are the insight in the sense of contemplation of impermanence, suffering, and non-self by means of breathing in and breathing out in each of the four bases of the first three tetrads.

VII. The Eight Kinds of Knowledge of Revulsion

276. Contemplating impermanence while breathing in, he knows and sees according to reality[96]—this is knowledge of revulsion. Contemplating impermanence while breathing out, he knows and sees according to reality—this is knowledge of revulsion ... (and so on, with the remaining six modes of the last tetrad).

VIII. The Eight Kinds of Knowledge in Conformity with Revulsion

277. The understanding of the appearance of fear[97] when contemplating impermanence while breathing in, is knowledge in conformity with revulsion. The understanding of the appearance of fear when contemplating impermanence while breathing out, is knowledge in conformity with revulsion ... (and so on, with the remaining six modes of the last tetrad).

IX. The Eight Kinds of Knowledge of Tranquillization of Revulsion

278. The understanding which is reflection and composure[98] when contemplating impermanence while breathing in, is knowledge of tranquillization of revulsion. The understanding which is reflection and composure when contemplating impermanence while breathing out, is knowledge of tranquillization of revulsion … (and so on, with the remaining six modes of the last tetrad).

X. The Twenty-one Kinds of Knowledge of the Bliss of Deliverance [99]

279. Knowledge of the bliss of deliverance arises because of the abandoning and cutting off by the path of stream-entry of—

    (i)   personality view,
    (ii)   uncertainty,
    (iii)   use of rites and rituals,
    (iv)   the inherent tendency to wrong view,
    (v)   the inherent tendency to uncertainty;

by the path of once return of—

    (vi)   the gross fetter of lust,
    (vii)   the gross fetter of aversion,
    (viii)   the gross inherent tendency to lust,
    (ix)   the gross inherent tendency to aversion;

by the path of non-return of—

    (x)   the residual fetter of lust,
    (xi)   the residual fetter of aversion,
    (xii)   the residual inherent tendency to lust,
    (xiii)   the residual inherent tendency to aversion;

by the path of arahatship of—

    (xiv)   greed for material existence,
    (xv)   greed for immaterial existence,

(xvi)   pride,
(xvii)   agitation,
(xviii)   ignorance,
(xix)   the inherent tendency to pride,
(xx)   the inherent tendency to greed for existence,
(xxi)   the inherent tendency to ignorance.

Part IV

PASSAGES FROM OTHER SUTTAS

From Vinaya Suttavibhaṅga, Pārājika III
(SN 54:9 gives a shorter version)

At one time, the Enlightened One, the Blessed One, was living at Vesālī in the Hall of the Gabled House in the Great Wood. At that time the Blessed One talked to the bhikkhus in many discourses on the foul.[1] He spoke in praise of the foul, he spoke variously in praise of attainment through the foul. Then the Blessed One addressed the bhikkhus thus, "I wish, bhikkhus, to go into retreat for a half-month. Let no one approach me except whoever brings almsfood."

"Even so, venerable sir," the bhikkhus replied to the Blessed One, and accordingly no one approached the Blessed One except whoever brought almsfood. Then, (thinking on what the Blessed One had said regarding the foul), those bhikkhus dwelt devoted to the practice of meditation on the foul in its many different aspects.

They became horrified by their own bodies, humiliated and revolted by them. Just as a woman or man—young, youthful, fond of ornaments, with head washed—would be horrified, humiliated, and revolted at having hung round her neck the carcase of a snake or a dog or a human being, so were those bhikkhus horrified, humiliated, and revolted by their own bodies. And they both took their own lives and took each other's lives.

Approaching Migalaṇḍika the sham recluse, they said, "It would be good, friend, if you would take our lives; then this bowl and robe would become yours." Then Migalaṇḍika the sham recluse, when he had taken the lives of many bhikkhus for the payment of a bowl and robe, came to the banks of the River Vaggumudā, carry-

ing a blood-stained knife. Then, while Migalaṇḍika the sham recluse was washing the blood-stained knife, he became sorry and re-
pentant, "Alas, for me that was loss and no gain; alas, for me that
was wrongly and not rightly come by; indeed, much demerit attaches to me because I took the lives of bhikkhus who were virtuous and well-conducted."

Then a certain deity of Māra's retinue came without cleaving
the water, and said to Migalaṇḍika the sham recluse, "Well done,
well done, good man; for you that was gain; for you that was rightly
come by; much merit attaches to you because you brought across
those who had not crossed."

The Migalaṇḍika the sham recluse (thought), "It is said that it is
gain for me; that it is rightly come by for me; that much merit
attaches to me because I brought across those who had not crossed";
and taking a sharp knife and going from monastery to monastery
and from cell to cell, he said, "Who has not crossed? Whom do I
bring across?" Thereupon those bhikkhus who were not rid of passion were paralysed with fear at that time, and their hair stood on
end. But those bhikkhus who were rid of passion were not paralysed by fear at that time, nor did their hair stand on end. Then
Migalaṇḍika the sham recluse, on a single day, took the life of one
bhikkhu, on a single day took the lives of two ... three ... four ...
five ... ten ... twenty ... thirty ... forty ... fifty ... sixty bhikkhus.

Now the Blessed One, on rising from his retreat at the end of
the half-month, addressed the Venerable Ānanda thus, "Why,
Ānanda, has the Order of bhikkhus become so reduced in number?"

"It is, venerable sir, because the Blessed One talked to the
bhikkhus in many discourses on the foul, spoke in praise of the
foul, spoke in praise of meditation on the foul, spoke variously in
praise of attainment through the foul. Then, venerable sir, (thinking on what the Blessed One has said regarding the foul), those
bhikkhus dwelt devoted to the practice of meditation on the foul in
its many different aspects. They became horrified by their own
bodies, humiliated and revolted by them (and he related all that

had taken place). It would be good, venerable sir, for the Blessed One to expound another discourse such that the Order of bhikkhus, knowing it, may become settled."

"Then, Ānanda, call together in the assembly hall as many bhikkhus as dwell near Vesāli."

"Even so, venerable sir," replied the Venerable Ānanda to the Blessed One. And then, when he had called together in the assembly hall as many bhikkhus as dwelt near Vesāli, he approached the Blessed One and said, "Venerable sir, the Order of bhikkhus is assembled; now is the time, venerable one, for the Blessed One to do as he thinks fit."

Then the Blessed One came to the assembly hall and sat down on the appointed seat. Having done so, the Blessed One addressed the bhikkhus:

"This respiration-mindfulness concentration, bhikkhus, developed and repeatedly practised, is both peaceful and sublime, unadulterated and of happy life; it causes to vanish at once and suppresses evil and unprofitable thoughts as soon as they arise.

"Just as, bhikkhus, in the last month of the hot season, the dirt and dust blow about, and then, out of season, a great rain cloud causes them to vanish at once and suppresses them; so, indeed, bhikkhus, respiration-mindfulness concentration, developed and repeatedly practised, is both peaceful and sublime, unadulterated and of happy life; it causes to vanish at once and suppresses evil and unprofitable thoughts as soon as they arise."

(Here follow the four tetrads as in MN 118, in Part I of this book.)

From Majjhima Nikāya, Sutta 62

"When, Rāhula, respiration-mindfulness is thus developed, thus repeatedly practised, the final in-breaths and out-breaths, too, (are) known (when) they cease, not unknown."

From Saṁyutta Nikāya 54

No. 4 Fruits I

"From respiration-mindfulness, bhikkhus, thus developed, thus repeatedly practised, one of two fruits is to be expected: final knowledge here and now, or, if there is some remainder of clinging, the state of non-return."

No. 5 Fruits II

"From respiration-mindfulness, bhikkhus, thus developed, thus repeatedly practised, seven fruits, seven benefits, are to be expected. What seven fruits, seven benefits?

  (i)   One attains to final knowledge here and now, in the course of life.

 (ii)   If one does not attain to final knowledge here and now, in the course of life, then one attains to final knowledge at the time of death.

(iii)   If one does not attain to final knowledge at the time of death, then, having destroyed the five lower fetters, (as a non-returner) one attains Nibbāna during (one's term of life in some particular heaven).

 (iv)   If one does not ... one attains Nibbāna after reducing (the number of rebirths).

  (v)   ... one attains Nibbāna without exertion.

 (vi)   ... one attains Nibbāna by exertion.

(vii)   ... one goes upstream, destined for the highest gods."

No. 6 Ariṭṭha

Thus have I heard. At one time the Blessed One was living at Sāvatthī, in Jeta's Grove, Anāthapiṇḍika's Park. There the Blessed One addressed the bhikkhus thus: "Bhikkhus."

"Venerable sir," the bhikkhus replied to the Blessed One. The Blessed One said this: "Do you, bhikkhus, practise respiration-mindfulness?"

When he had spoken thus, the Venerable Ariṭṭha said to the Blessed One: "I, venerable sir, practise respiration-mindfulness?"

"And how, Ariṭṭha, do you practise respiration-mindfulness?"

"In me, venerable sir, greed for past sense pleasures is abandoned; in me, greed for future sense pleasures is departed; in me, perception of aversion concerning things internal and external is entirely put away.[2] Mindful I shall breathe in, mindful I shall breathe out. Thus, venerable one, do I practise respiration-mindfulness."

"This respiration-mindfulness, Ariṭṭha, exists; it is not non-existent, I say. Moreover, Ariṭṭha, hear how this respiration-mindfulness is fulfilled in detail, and attend carefully to what I shall say." (Here follow the four tetrads.)

No. 7   Kappina

Thus have I heard. At one time the Blessed One was living at Sāvatthī, in Jeta's Grove, Anāthapiṇḍika's Park.

At that time the Venerable Mahā-Kappina was seated not far off, having folded his legs crosswise, set his body erect, and established mindfulness in front of him.

Then the Blessed One, seeing the Venerable Mahā-Kappina thus seated, addressed the bhikkhus thus: "Have you, bhikkhus, observed any wavering or trembling of body in this bhikkhu?"

"Whenever we have seen him, venerable sir, whether seated amid the Order, or seated alone and secluded, we have never observed any wavering or trembling of body in that venerable one."

"That concentration, bhikkhus, from the development and the repeated practice of which there comes to be neither wavering nor trembling of body, nor wavering nor trembling of mind—that bhikkhu is one who obtains such concentration at will, without difficulty, and in full.

"And from the development, bhikkhus, from the repeated practice, of what concentration does there come to be neither wavering nor trembling of body, nor wavering nor trembling of mind? From the development, from the repeated practice, of respiration-mindfulness concentration, there comes to be neither wavering nor trembling of body, nor wavering nor trembling of mind."

No. 8   The Lamp

Thus have I heard. At one time the Blessed One was living at Sāvatthī, in Jeta's Grove, Anāthapiṇḍika's Park. There the Blessed One addressed the bhikkhus thus: "Bhikkhus."

"Venerable sir," the bhikkhus replied to the Blessed One. The Blessed One said this: "Respiration-mindfulness concentration, bhikkhus, developed and repeatedly practised, is of great fruit, of great benefit. And how developed, bhikkhus, how repeatedly practised, is respiration-mindfulness concentration of great fruit, of great benefit?

(Repeat the four tetrads.)

"Thus developed, bhikkhus, thus repeatedly practised, respiration-mindfulness concentration is of great fruit, of great benefit.

"Before my enlightenment, bhikkhus, while I was still only an unenlightened Bodhisatta, I too dwelt much in this way of life. Dwelling much in this way of life, neither my body nor my eyes became fatigued,[3] and through not clinging, my mind was freed from the cankers.

"Therefore, bhikkhus, if a bhikkhu should desire, 'May neither my body nor my eyes become fatigued and through not clinging may my mind be freed from the cankers,' let him reflect well upon this respiration-mindfulness concentration.

"Therefore, bhikkhus, if a bhikkhu should desire, 'Whatever my memories and thoughts based on the household life, may they be abandoned,' let him …

"Therefore, bhikkhus, if a bhikkhu should desire, 'May I dwell perceiving the repugnant in the unrepugnant,' let him ...

"Therefore, bhikkhus, if a bhikkhu should desire, 'May I dwell perceiving the unrepugnant in the repugnant,' let him ...

"Therefore, bhikkhus, if a bhikkhu should desire, 'May I dwell perceiving the repugnant in the unrepugnant and the repugnant,' let him ...

"Therefore, bhikkhus, if a bhikkhu should desire, 'May I dwell perceiving the unrepugnant in the repugnant and the unrepugnant,' let him ...

"Therefore, bhikkhus, if a bhikkhu should desire, 'Avoiding both the unrepugnant and the repugnant, may I dwell indifferent, mindful, clearly comprehending,' let him ...

"Therefore, bhikkhus, if a bhikkhu should desire, 'Aloof from sense-desires, aloof from unprofitable thoughts, having entered upon the first jhāna, which is accompanied by applied and sustained thought and is filled with rapture and bliss born of seclusion, may I dwell therein,' let him ...

"Therefore, bhikkhus, if a bhikkhu should desire, 'Through the subsiding of applied and sustained thought, having entered upon the second jhāna, which is possessed of internal calm and single-ness of mind, and is without applied thought and without sustained thought, and is filled with rapture and bliss born of concentration, may I dwell therein,' let him ...

"Therefore, bhikkhus, if a bhikkhu should desire, 'Through the fading away of rapture may I dwell indifferent, mindful and clearly comprehending, and experience through the mental faculties that bliss of which the noble ones say, "He who is indifferent and mindful dwells happily," having entered upon the third jhāna, may I dwell therein,' let him ...

"Therefore, bhikkhus, if a bhikkhu should desire, 'Through the abandoning of bodily bliss and the abandoning of bodily pain, and through the disappearance of previous joy and grief, having en-tered upon the fourth jhāna which is neither painful nor pleasant and is possessed of mindfulness purified by indifference, may I abide therein,' let him ...

"Therefore, bhikkhus, if a bhikkhu should desire, 'From the complete surmounting of perceptions of materiality, from the disappearance of perceptions of resistance, from non-attention to perceptions of variety, (aware that) "boundless is space," having entered upon the sphere of boundless space, may I dwell therein,' let him ...

"Therefore, bhikkhus, if a bhikkhu should desire, 'From the complete surmounting of the sphere of boundless space, (aware that) "boundless is consciousness," having entered upon the sphere of boundless consciousness, may I dwell therein,' let him ...

"Therefore, bhikkhus, if a bhikkhu should desire, 'From the complete surmounting of the sphere of boundless consciousness, (aware that) "there is nothing," having entered upon the sphere of nothingness, may I dwell therein,' let him ...

"Therefore, bhikkhus, if a bhikkhu should desire, 'From the complete surmounting of the sphere of nothingness, having entered upon the sphere of neither-perception-nor-non-perception, may I dwell therein,' let him ...

"Therefore, bhikkhus, if a bhikkhu should desire, 'From the entire overcoming of the sphere of neither-perception-nor-non-perception, having entered upon the cessation of perception and feeling, may I dwell therein,' let him reflect well upon this respiration-mindfulness concentration.

"When respiration-mindfulness concentration is thus developed, thus repeatedly practised, if he experiences a pleasant feeling, he understands, 'That is impermanent'; he understands 'That is not seized upon'; he understands, 'That is not assimilated.' If he experiences a painful feeling, he understands, 'That is impermanent'; he understands, 'That is not seized upon'; he understands, 'That is not assimilated.' If he experiences a neither-pleasant-nor-painful feeling, he understands, 'That is impermanent'; he understands, 'That is not seized upon'; he understands, 'That is not assimilated.'

"If he experiences a pleasant feeling, he experiences it as one dissociated from it. If he experiences a painful feeling, he experiences it as one dissociated from it. If he experiences a neither-pleasant-nor-painful feeling, he experiences it as one dissociated from it.

"Experiencing a feeling of the body coming to its end, he understands, 'I experience a feeling of the body coming to its end.' Experiencing a feeling of life coming to its end, he understands, 'I experience a feeling of life coming to its end.' He understands, 'On the breakup of the body, after the end of life, all experiences, from being not assimilated, will grow cold.'

"Suppose, bhikkhus, a lamp were burning because of oil and a wick, but if the oil and the wick came to an end, the lamp would go out through lack of nutriment, so, indeed, bhikkhus, (when) a bhikkhu experiences a feeling of the body coming to its end, he understands, 'I experience a feeling of the body coming to its end.' Experiencing a feeling of life coming to its end, he understands, 'I experience a feeling of life coming to its end.' He understands, 'On the breakup of the body, after the end of life, all experiences, from being not assimilated, will grow cold.' "

No. 10 Kimbila

"Suppose, Ānanda, there were a large heap of rubbish at the four crossroads, and a cart or carriage came from an easterly ... or a westerly ... or a northerly ... or a southerly direction, it would demolish that heap of rubbish. So, indeed, Ānanda, a bhikkhu who dwells contemplating the body in the body ... the feelings in the feelings ... the mind in the mind ... mental objects in mental objects, demolishes evil, unprofitable thoughts."

No. 11 At Icchānangala

Thus have I heard. At one time the Blessed One was living at Icchānangala in the Forest Grove of Icchānangala.

Then the Blessed One addressed the bhikkhus thus, "I wish, bhikkhus, to go into retreat for three months. Let no one approach me except whoever brings almsfood."

"Even so, venerable sir," the bhikkhus replied to the Blessed One. And accordingly no one approached the Blessed One except whoever brought almsfood.

Then the Blessed One, on rising from his retreat at the end of the three months, addressed the bhikkhus:

"If, bhikkhus, the wandering ascetics of other sects ask you thus: 'In what way of life, friend, does the recluse Gotama mainly dwell during the residence of the rains?', you, bhikkhus, being questioned thus, should reply to those wandering ascetics of other sects thus: 'In respiration-mindfulness concentration, friends, does the recluse Gotama mainly dwell during the residence of the rains.'

(Here follow the four tetrads, but in the first person.)

"Were it, bhikkhus, rightly speaking to be said of anything, 'This is the life of the noble ones, this is the life of purity, this is the life of the Tathāgata,' it is of respiration-mindfulness concentration, indeed, that rightly speaking it should be said, 'This is that (kind of) life.'

"Those bhikkhus who as trainees dwell with their ideal as yet unattained, aspiring to the supreme surcease of bondage, for them respiration-mindfulness concentration, developed and repeatedly practised, leads to the destruction of the cankers. And those bhikkhus who are arahats, in whom the cankers are destroyed, who have lived the life, done what is to be done, laid down the burden, reached the highest good, destroyed the fetters of becoming, who knowing rightly are delivered, for them respiration-mindfulness concentration, developed and repeatedly practised, leads to a happy life here and now and to mindfulness and clear comprehension.

"Were it, bhikkhus, rightly speaking to be said of anything, 'This is the life of the noble ones, this is the life of purity, this is the life of the Tathāgata'; it is of respiration-mindfulness concentration, indeed, that rightly speaking it should be said, 'This is that (kind of) life.' "

No. 17

"Respiration-mindfulness concentration, bhikkhus, developed and repeatedly practised, leads to the abandoning of the fetters."

No. 18

"... leads to the abolishing of the inherent tendencies."

No. 19

" ... leads to knowledge of the life-term."

No. 20

" ... leads to the destruction of the cankers."

From Aṅguttara Nikāya

Ekaka Nipāta, 16

"One thing, bhikkhus, developed and repeatedly practised, leads to complete revulsion, to fading away, to cessation, to pacification, to direct knowledge, to enlightenment, to Nibbāna. What is this one thing? Respiration-mindfulness."

Pañcaka Nipāta, 96

"Possessed, bhikkhus, of five things, a bhikkhu practising respiration-mindfulness penetrates the immovable after no long time. Which five?

"Here, bhikkhus, a bhikkhu: (i) undertakes little, has few duties, is easily supported, well contented with the necessities of life; (ii) he takes little food, is not addicted to filling his stomach; (iii) he is not torpid, and is devoted to wakefulness; (iv) he is well versed and remembers what he has learned and as to those things that are good in the beginning, good in the middle, good in the end, and that with the meaning and the letter set forth the life of purity which is quite perfected and purified—those things he learns well, bears in mind, recites verbally, considers with his mind, and thoroughly penetrates with vision; (v) he reviews his mind as to how far it is liberated.

"Possessed, bhikkhus, of these five things, a bhikkhu practising respiration-mindfulness penetrates the immovable in no long time."

No. 97
(Repeat the foregoing, substituting for (iv) the ten kinds of talk in Aṅguttara, Navaka Nipāta 1, second paragraph—see p.105).

No. 98
(Repeat the foregoing, substituting for (iv): "he is one who lives in the forest and maintains a secluded abode.")

From Chakka Nipāta, 115

"There are, bhikkhus, these three things. Which three? Unruly speech, bad friendship, distraction of the mind. These, bhikkhus, are the three things.

"For the abandoning, bhikkhus, of those three things, three things are to be developed. Which three?

"For the abandoning of unruly speech, gentle speech is to be developed. For the abandoning of bad friendship, good friendship is to be developed. For the abandoning of distraction of the mind, respiration-mindfulness is to be developed. For the abandoning, bhikkhus, of those three things, these three things are to be developed."

From Navaka Nipāta, 1 (= Udāna, IV, 1)

"Of a bhikkhu, bhikkhus, who has a good friend, a good companion, a good intimate, this is to be expected: he will dwell possessed of virtue, possessed of the Pāṭimokkha[4] restraint, with good conduct as his domain; and seeing fear in the smallest fault, he will train himself by undertaking the precepts of training.

"Of a bhikkhu, bhikkhus, who has a good friend, a good companion, a good intimate, this is to be expected: such talk as is concerned with effacement, as favours the mind's liberation—that is to say, talk on wanting little, on contentment, seclusion, aloofness from contact, strenuousness, virtuous conduct, concentration, understanding, deliverance, knowledge and vision concerning deliverance—he will be one who gains such talk at will, without difficulty and in full.

"Of a bhikkhu, bhikkhus, who has a good friend, a good companion, a good intimate, this is to be expected: he will live applying himself energetically to the giving up of whatever is bad, and to the taking hold of whatever is good; he will be firm and unwavering in his efforts, never laying aside the pursuit of the good.

"Of a bhikkhu, bhikkhus, who has a good friend, a good companion, a good intimate, this is to be expected: he will dwell possessed of understanding, endowed with the understanding that sees rise and fall, that is noble, penetrative, and leads to the entire destruction of suffering.

"But, bhikkhus, four things should be developed as well by the bhikkhu who has become established in these five things.[5] The foul is to be developed for the abandoning of lust; amity is to be developed for the abandoning of ill will; respiration-mindfulness is to be developed for the cutting off of thoughts; perception of impermanence is to be developed for the destruction of the pride that says 'I am.' For a bhikkhu who perceives impermanence, bhikkhus, perception of non-self is established; one who perceives non-self reaches the destruction of the pride that says 'I am,' that is, Nibbāna here and now."

Itivuttaka 85

"Dwell, bhikkhus, contemplating the foul in the body, and let mindfulness of your own respiration be well established before you. Dwell contemplating impermanence in all formations. For those who dwell contemplating the foul in the body, the inherent tendency to lust regarding the element of beauty is abandoned. When mindfulness of one's own respiration is well established before one, the habits of thought which tend to produce irritation are no more. For those who dwell contemplating impermanence in all formations, ignorance is abandoned and clear vision arises.

> "In the body the foul discerning,
> Mindful of breathing in and out,
> Ever ardent, comprehending
> Pacification of all formations.
>
> Indeed, this bhikkhu rightly seeing
> Is henceforth liberated here;
> Armed with full knowledge and at peace
> This sage has severed all bonds."

Notes

Part I: The Discourse on Respiration-mindfulness

1. "Distinction" is used here in the sense of attainment or progress. "After the earlier distinction due to perfection of virtue, etc., they realized further distinction through preliminary contemplation-device practice, etc." (Paps).

2. The Pavāraṇā ceremony is held at the end of the rainy season, during which season bhikkhus are obliged to undertake to reside in one dwelling for three months. It consists of an assembly of bhikkhus at which each member present invites (*pavāreti*) the Order to point out his faults committed during the preceding period. It is normally held at the end of the first three months of the rains (in the month of Assayuja = October), but can be postponed, as in this case, till a month later (i.e. the month of Kattika = November). The full-moon day is the last day of the month. For details see Vin I 157–78 and Paps I 93, II 150.

3. Namely, arahatship.

4. *Komudi* is the full moon of the month of Kattika, called Komudi on account of white water lilies (*kumuda*) said to blossom then. Cf. also Dhp 285.

5. *Suddhā, sāre patiṭṭhitā*: the same phrase occurs at MN I 25 and I 488, where it is used in the simile of removal of sappy wood, etc., leaving only the heartwood.

6. The ten fetters (*saṃyojana*) are: (i) belief in a self, (ii) uncertainty, (iii) belief in rites and rituals, (iv) lust, (v) ill will, (vi) greed for fine-material existence, (vii) greed for immaterial existence, (viii) pride, (ix) agitation, (x) ignorance. The first five are the "lower" (*orambhāgiya*) fetters, which bind beings to rebirth in the sense-desire world; the second five are the "higher" (*uddhambhāgiya*) fetters, which bind beings to rebirth in the fine-material and immaterial worlds.

7. The first three of the aforesaid fetters.

8. See MN No. 10.

9. The efforts to restrain and abandon the unprofitable, and the efforts to develop and maintain the profitable. See DN No. 33 and MN No. 141.

10. Or bases of success (*iddhipāda*). They are: concentration of zeal, with the will to give this precedence; concentration of energy...; concentration of (purity of) consciousness...; concentration of investigation, with the will to give this precedence. See MN No. 16 and DN No. 33.

11. The faculties of faith (or confidence), energy, mindfulness, concentration, and understanding—"faculty" in the sense of predominance. See SN V 201.

12. The same five as for the faculties, but "power" in the sense of unshakability. See SN V 219.

13. The enlightenment factors of mindfulness, investigation-of-states, energy, rapture, tranquillity, concentration, and equanimity. See SN V 63.

14. From the "four foundations of mindfulness" to the "eight path factors" are what are known in the commentaries as "the thirty-seven states partaking of enlightenment."

15. This and the previous three are known as the "four divine abodes." See MN I 38, Vism, Ch. IX.

16. The meditation on the foul (*asubha*) consists of the nine "cemetery contemplations," or the contemplation of the parts of the body, given at MN I 58. See also Vism. Ch. VI, VIII.

17. "Here insight is meant by perception" (Paps).

18. For "bodily formation" and "mental formation" see MN I 301: "In-and-out breathing, Visākha, are the bodily formation; applied and sustained thought are the verbal formation; and feeling and perception are the mental formation." For this tetrad, compare MN I 56, where there is added the simile of the turner: "Just as a skilled turner or turner's apprentice, making a long turn, knows, 'I make a long turn,' or making a short turn knows, 'I make a short turn.' "

19. There is no satisfactory rendering of the word *pīti*. "Absorbing interest" is too limited; "rapture" has the disadvantage of its association with Western mysticism, but is probably the least unsatis-

factory. In the commentaries, *pīti* is compared to what is felt by an exhausted traveller on seeing cool water ahead, while *sukha* (bliss) is compared to his feeling when enjoying the cool water.

20. *Virāga* also has no satisfactory rendering. *Rāga* (originally meaning "colour," "dye") is used for "greed" or "lust"; *virāga* is the fading away of the colour, the disappearance of greed or lust. It occurs frequently in the suttas in the sequence *nibbidā, virāga, nirodha, paṭinissagga*, i.e. revulsion (or turning away from the round of rebirths), dispassion (or fading away of greed), cessation, relinquishment.

21. These four tetrads are found also at MN I 425, at AN V 111, in many suttas in SN No. 54, and at Ps I 95.

22. "Herein what is 'the world'? That very body is the world, and the five aggregates (as objects) of clinging are the world; this is called the world" (Vbh 195, *Satipaṭṭhāna Vibhaṅga*).

23. *Nirāmisa*, "not of the flesh." On the subject of *āmisa* and *nirāmisa* see MN I 12, 59; Paps I 89, 279.

24. For B, C, and D, repeat (1)–(7) of A.

Part II: The Commentary on the Sutta

1. The material up to here has been adapted from Vism. The passage "is of great fruit" to "supramundane bliss is of great benefit" is taken, for completeness, from Paps I 159. What follows is from Vism without adaptation. Only certain long quotations from Ps have been replaced by references to the Ps passages given in Part III.

2. Also, AN II 238. Paps II 4, quoting AN II 238f. in support, gives the following: "The recluse is a stream-enterer, the second recluse is a once-returner, the third recluse is a non-returner, the fourth recluse is an arahat." Paps, commenting on MN No.122, also remarks that the four paths of holiness are not found outside the Buddha's dispensation. Also Pm 257 has the following: " 'For the person who produces respiration-mindfulness concentration in all its aspects' means the grasping of all aspects with reference to the sixteen bases; these exist only in this dispensation, although those outside the dispensation who are endowed with knowledge know the (first) four bases only."

3. As noted in Vism translation (*Path of Purification*), the word *kūṭa*
    must here mean "vicious," "wild," or some such quality; not given
    in PTS Dict.

4. These are two stages of concentration. "Access concentration"
    (*upacāra-samādhi*) approaches, but does not reach the "full ab-
    sorption" (*appanā-samādhi*) achieved in jhāna.

5. So Pm 257.

6. AN V 135: "For one delighting in seclusion, delight in society is a
    thorn; for one devoted to contemplation of the foul, the sign of the
    beautiful is a thorn; for one guarding the doors of the sense facul-
    ties, the seeing of shows is a thorn; for one who leads the life of
    purity, consorting with women is a thorn; for the first jhāna, noise
    is a thorn; for the second jhāna, applied and sustained thought are
    a thorn; for the third jhāna, rapture is a thorn; for the fourth jhāna,
    in-and-out breathing is a thorn; for the attainment of the cessation
    of perception and feeling, perception and feeling are a thorn. Greed
    is a thorn, hate is a thorn, delusion is a thorn. Dwell thornless,
    bhikkhus, dwell free from thorns, bhikkhus. Dwell thornless and
    free from thorns, bhikkhus. Thornless, bhikkhus, are the arahats;
    free from thorns, bhikkhus, are the arahats; thornless and free from
    thorns, bhikkhus, are the arahats."

7. Cf. DN I 9, 12; II 87.

8. *Indakhīla*: "Indra's post," the post, stake, column of Indra at, or
    before, any city gate; also a large slab of stone let into the ground
    at the entrance of a house (PTS Dict.).

9. The vicinity (of a tree) means "where at midday full shadow is
    cast, or (within the area) where, when it is calm, leaves (from it)
    fall, that area is termed 'the root of a tree'; in this sense it is said
    'the vicinity of a tree' " (Pm 258).

10. "The remaining seven kinds of abode being a hill, a rock cleft, a
    mountain cave, a charnel ground, a forest thicket, an open space,
    and a heap of straw" (Pm 258; see MN I 181).

11. " 'An abode suitable to the three seasons,' etc.: the three seasons
    beginning with the hot season; the three humours of the body
    beginning with the phlegmatic; the three kinds of temperament be-
    ginning with the deluded temperament. So, indeed, in the hot sea-

son, the forest is favourable; in the cold season, the root of a tree; in the rainy season, an empty place. For one of phlegmatic humour, phlegmatic by nature, the forest is favourable; for one of irritable (bilious) humour, the root of a tree; for one of windy humour, an empty place. For one of deluded temperament, the forest; for one of angry temperament, the root of a tree; for one of sensual temperament, an empty place" (Pm 258).

12. "For him there is no producing of in- (or out-) breathing unaccompanied by mindfulness—'he is one who practises mindfulness': he is so because of doing, by being mindful only, what should be done only with mindfulness; or he has the habit of so doing. Why is it that in the analysis of the passage, 'mindful he breathes in, mindful he breathes out,' instead of saying simply 'he breathes in, he breathes out,' 'one who practises mindfulness' is stated? It is owing to the wish to make the teaching consistent. For in the beginning of the first tetrad the meaning is expressed in the present tense; in the rest it is in the future tense. That is why the expression 'one who practises mindfulness' is used throughout in this paragraph owing to the wish to make the teaching consistent" (Pm 259).

13. There is uncertainty as to whether *ānam* and *assāso* mean breathing in, and *apānam* and *passāso* breathing out, or *vice versa*. Here, the former rendering is adopted throughout. "According to the Vinaya interpretation breath originating within is *assāsa*: breath originating without is *passāso*. According to the Suttanta interpretation, however, *assāso* (refers to) breath inside the body having originated outside; *passāso* (refers to) breath outside, having originated outside" (Pm 259).

14. This passage is quoted in full in Vism at this point but is omitted here and will be found in the Ps section under "long" and "short" breaths. (See pp.68–70, paras. 12–13, where the "nine ways" are given.)

15. "Diffused on account of the state of being broken up into minute particles of many groups" (Pm 262), i.e. regarded as successive arisings.

16. " 'In the early (stage of the) method' means in the early stage of the method of development; in the first two of the sixteen bases, is

what is intended. And it is there, certainly, that knowledge is found to arise owing to the presence of the correct understanding of length and shortness of the in-breaths and out-breaths. And, according as that is not hard to do, that is, the mere taking of the breaths as they occur, it is put in the present tense (in the text). But what follows is as hard as for a man to walk on a razor's edge; that is why the future tense is used (for the subsequent stages), in order to illustrate the need there for an outstanding store of previously accumulated merit and, so as to point this meaning out, he said, 'herein because,' and so on" (Pm 263).

17. That is, when starting contemplation (see n.16).

18. The four elements: earth, water, fire, and air.

19. The twenty-four kinds of derived materiality are: eye, ear, nose, tongue, body-sensitivity; visible object, sound, odour, taste; femininity, masculinity, physical base of mind, bodily intimation, verbal intimation, vitality, space; physical agility, elasticity, tractability, growth, continuity, decay, impermanence; nutrition.

20. Impermanence, suffering, and non-self (*anicca, dukkha, anattā*).

21. "By the method stated in the method of tranquillity beginning with the words, 'at the time of not discerning '" (Pm 264).

22. The simile of the gong with its objection and reply is quoted in Vism at this point, but is omitted here as it is contained in the Ps section (see pp.77–78, para 60).

23. Analysis of meaning, of law, of word formation, of clear expression. See AN II 160, Vism XIV, 21–26.

24. (a) Virtue according to Pātimokkha restraint; (b) virtue as restraint of the controlling faculties by guarding the senses; (c) abstinence from wrong livelihood; (d) the use of the four requisites after proper reflection. See Vism I, 42.

25. See Vism III, 29–56.

26. See AN IV 85–87.

27. See MN I 37.

28. Vimm has the following: "Here, 'he trains himself in breathing in (and out)' means mindfulness is fixed at the nose-tip or the upper lip. These are the places connected with the breathing in and out.

The yogin attends to the incoming (and outgoing) breath there. He considers the contact of the incoming and the outgoing breath through mindfulness which is fixed at the nose-tip or on the upper lip. Mindful he breathes in, mindful he breathes out. He does not consider the breath when it has gone inside nor when it has gone outside. He considers the contact of the incoming breath and the outgoing breath at the nose-tip or on the upper lip with mindfulness. He breathes in and breathes out with mindfulness. It is as if a man were sawing wood. That man does not attend to the going back and forth of the saw. In the same way, the yogin does not attend to the perception of the (coming and going) of the incoming and outgoing breaths in respiration-mindfulness. He is aware of the contact at the nose-tip or on the upper lip and he breathes in and out with mindfulness. If, when the breath comes in or goes out, the yogin considers it within or without, his mind will be distracted. If his mind is distracted, his body and mind will waver and tremble. These are the disadvantages. He should not purposely breathe very long or very short breaths. If (he does) so, his mind will be distracted (as aforesaid). (Note: This last is a point which does not seem to be made in Vism.) He should not attach himself to diverse perceptions connected with breathing in and breathing out. If (he does) so, his other mental factors will be disturbed. If his mind is disturbed, his body and mind will waver and tremble. Thus, countless impediments arise because the points of contact of the incoming and the outgoing breath (all along their course) are countless. He should be recollected and should not let the mind be distracted. He should not try too strenuously nor too lazily. If he tries too lazily, he will fall into stiffness-and-torpor. If he tries too strenuously, he will become restless."

29. Vimm has the following: "Certain of the Ancients taught four ways of practising mindfulness as to respiration. They are counting, connection, contacting (or touching), and fixing."

30. Vimm has the following: "A new yogin counts the breaths from one to ten, beginning with the outgoing breath and ending with the incoming breath. He does not count beyond ten. Again, it is taught that he counts from one to five, but does not count beyond five. He does not miss (a breath). If he does, he should count the next or stop that count. Thus he dwells in mindfulness as to in-breathing

and out-breathing, attending to the object. Thus should counting be understood. Counting suppresses uncertainty; it causes the abandoning of uncertainty."

31.   Pm 267.

32.   "This is said referring to one to whom only one of the two, i.e. in-breath or out-breath, becomes manifest; but one to whom both become manifest should do his counting taking both together. And the meaning expressed by the words, 'that ... manifest' should be regarded as: of the wind in the two nostrils, that which is manifested more plainly should be taken" (Pm 267–68).

33.   Pm 268.

34.   Pm 268.

35.   Pm 268 comments: "'One, two, three, four, five,' show the manner of counting. Therefore, in saying 'eight,' and so on, eight and so on are to be reached separately beginning from one."

36.   Passage not clear. Pm 268 merely says: "To one who reflects much on breath gone inside, that place seems as though struck by the wind or filled with fat; thus it appears." The meaning might perhaps be that he feels the impact of the wind of the breath inside his body, which is felt as though his lungs were filled with a solid substance.

37.   Since there are various interpretations of how the counting should actually be done, it is worthwhile mentioning the following points here (although this matter seems disproportionately overwritten already): (a) the unit, for counting purposes, can be taken as: "one"—in-breath and out-breath; or "one"—out-breath and in-breath; or "one"—in-breath, and "two"—out-breath; or "one"—out-breath, and "two"—in-breath; (b) when a maximum number between five and ten has been decided upon, count from one up to that number and begin again. An alternative method is to count from one to five, then from one to six, one to seven, one to eight, one to nine, one to ten, and begin again. (c) "Counting slowly like a grain-measurer" and "counting quickly like a cowherd" should not be understood as a speeding up of the breaths by deliberately causing a change in their rhythm. This is the stage of bare observation and there is no active control of the breath, but merely the watching and noting of it as it proceeds. If it speeds up or slows down "of itself," this is

merely noted. "Counting slowly," therefore, means waiting at each count till the breath unit is finished before registering the count, as the grain-measurer goes on saying "one" till the moment comes to empty his second basket. This is the initial stage. When some facility has been reached, and consciousness is less inclined to stray, the "counting quickly" can be done at the beginning of the breath-unit. Thus, consciousness becomes less intent upon the numbers and more so on the breaths themselves.

38. "Having caused the arising of air-perception, he dwells attending to the contact of the incoming and the outgoing breath at the nose-tip or the upper lip" (Vimm). Does this refer to the "air kasiṇa"? At Vism III, 119, it is said: "respiration-mindfulness is to be grasped by touch, the air kasiṇa is to be grasped by sight and touch, the remaining nine kasiṇas by sight." Atthasālinī, p. 200, has: "Respiration-jhāna is included in the air kasiṇa."

39. Pm 268 comments: "'Following' is the proceeding closely after with mindfulness by making each arising of in-breathing and out-breathing the object (of consciousness); therefore, he says, in fact, 'he should not follow the beginning, middle, and end.'"

40. Pm 268 comments: "'The navel is the beginning' here because of first arising. For the concept of beginning is here in the sense of first (of a series of) arisings, not in the sense of merely (one) arising. For they arise accordingly, (successively) throughout the length from the navel up to the nose-tip. Wherever they arise, there they break up, because of the absence of anything that moves; but the notion of movement is in regard to (successive) arisings within a (given) space according to conditions. 'The heart (is) the middle': near the heart; the middle is its upper part. 'The nose-tip is the end': the place where the nose is, is its end, because the notion of in-breathing and out-breathing does not extend beyond that, since they are stated as 'originated by mind' and there is no producing of anything mind-originated outside (that point)."

41. Quotation is given in full here. In the Ps translation which follows it is compressed.

42. "Having acquired facility in contacting, he should establish the sign and he should establish rapture, bliss, and the other jhāna factors which arise here" (Vimm).

43. Pm 269 comments: "Without counting and connection there is no
    giving attention to the meditation subject by way of contact and by
    way of fixing alone in their due turn. Is it not a fact, then, that
    there is also no bringing to mind by counting without contact, just
    as there is no fixing without contact? Even if there is not, counting
    has still to be taken as the first condition, because of its being the
    root condition for bringing the meditation subject to mind. So with
    connection (in relation) to fixing, without that (connection) there is
    no state of fixing. Therefore, as there exists an uninterrupted state
    of contact, just because of having taken counting and connection
    by way of first condition through being the root condition, there is
    no (separate attention) to the others (i.e. contact and fixing). Point-
    ing this out, he said, 'There is, in fact, no attention to be given to it
    by contact separate from fixing, as there is by counting and con-
    nection.' If (this is) so, why are they enumerated separately, say-
    ing 'just there at the point of contact' and so on? Here, saying
    'counting ... at the point of contact,' he thereby points out that
    contact is a factor of counting; therefore he says 'he brings to mind
    by way of counting and contact.' "

44. Pm 270.

45. Beginning, middle, and end is said here in the sense of not missing
    any part of the breaths as they pass the nose-tip, thus maintaining
    continuous mindfulness. There is no conflict, therefore, with the
    warning (given elsewhere) against following the beginning, mid-
    dle, and end by leaving the nose-tip to follow after the breaths
    inside or outside the body.

46. "Counting suppresses uncertainty. It causes the abandoning of un-
    certainty. Connection removes gross applied thought and causes
    unbroken mindfulness as to in-and-out breathing. Contacting re-
    moves distraction and makes for steady perception. He attains to
    distinction through bliss (in fixing)" (Vimm).

47. "To the yogin who attends (to the breath) with a mind that is
    cleansed of the nine lesser defilements, the sign arises with a pleasant
    feeling similar to that felt while spinning cotton. Also, it is likened
    to the pleasant feeling produced by a breeze. Thus, in breathing in
    and out, air touches the nose-tip and causes the establishment of
    mindfulness of air perception. This does not depend on colour or

form. This is called the sign. If the yogin develops the sign and increases it through repeated practice, increases it at the nose-tip, between the eyebrows, on the forehead, or establishes it in several places, he feels as if his head were filled with air. Through increasing it in this way, his whole body is charged with bliss. This is called perfection" (Vimm). However, Vism III, 113, speaking of signs which should and should not be increased, says: "He who increases the respiration sign only increases the accumulation of wind and it is limited in locality."

48. "The counterpart sign" (Pm 271).

49. The jhāna factors are: applied thought, sustained thought, rapture, bliss, equanimity.

50. This passage has been translated differently elsewhere, but the sense seems clear; the lesson taught is that given at MN III 112: "...He brings to mind the imperturbable (four arūpa jhānas). (Although) bringing to mind the imperturbable, still his mind does not enter the imperturbable nor does it become settled, steady, and resolute. When that is so, Ānanda, the bhikkhu understands (that that is so). Thus he is possessed of clear comprehension therein. By that, Ānanda, his mind should (then continue to be) internally settled, steadied, unified, and concentrated in the same sign of concentration as before." Cf. MN No.128.

51. Pm 273 comments: "The acquired sign (*uggahanimitta*), and the counterpart sign (*paṭibhāganimitta*), for both are stated here together. For herein, the similes beginning with the 'tuft of cotton' apply to the acquired sign; the remainder to both signs.... The similes beginning with 'like a round gem or a round pearl' apply to the counterpart sign." It is not stated on what grounds this division is based. Vimm in this connection says: "And again there is a yogin who sees several signs from the beginning such as smoke, dust, gold-dust, or he experiences something like the pricking of a needle or an ant's bite. If his mind does not become clear regarding these different signs he will be confused; thus he does not gain perception of in-and-out breathing. If his mind becomes clear, the yogin does not experience confusion; he attends to the incoming and outgoing breaths and he does not cause the arising of other perceptions. Meditating thus, he is able to end confusion and ac-

quire the subtle sign. And he attends to the incoming breath and
the outgoing breath with a mind that is free. Because that sign is
free, virtuous desire arises. Virtuous desire being free, that yogin
attends to the incoming breath and the outgoing breath and becomes joyful. Virtuous desire and joy being free, he attends to the
incoming breath and the outgoing breath and becomes indifferent.
Indifference, virtuous desire, and joy being free, he attends to the
incoming breath and the outgoing breath and his mind is not disturbed. If his mind is not disturbed he will destroy the hindrances
and arouse the jhāna factors. Thus this yogin will reach the calm
and sublime fourth jhāna."

52. Pm 274.

53. "Counterpart sign" (Pm 274).

54. "*Vibhāvayaṃ*"—either "causing to vanish" or "making known."
    Pm 274 comments: "Vibhāvayaṃ: causing to vanish; causing to
    disappear. Since the arising of the sign these aspects are as though
    made to vanish for one who does not bring them to mind .... But
    there are those who say the meaning is: ' *Vibhāvayaṃ* is causing to
    be manifest, making known, plain'; the meaning should then be
    construed as the preliminary stage (of concentration)."

55. DN III 59–60.

56. Paps IV 162, commenting on MN No. 122, says: "This bhikkhu's
    tranquillity and insight are fresh, and for the purpose of guarding
    them:

    > 'Abode, resort, and speech, and person,
    > The food, the climate, and the posture:
    > (Select and) cultivate of each
    > The kind that is most suitable.'

    These seven kinds of suitability are desirable."

57. See Vism IV 42–66.

58. See Vism IV 198–202. Here the fivefold instead of the fourfold
    classification of jhānas is used, dividing the first into two, i.e. with
    applied and sustained thought; and with sustained thought only.

59. Adverting to, entering upon, deciding upon duration, emerging, re-
    viewing; see Vism IV 131–32.

60. Pm 375 comments: "'With the arising of ignorance there is the arising of materiality (Ps I 55), and so forth; he investigates (and) scrutinizes it as having its beginning in ignorance."

61. See Vism, Chap. XIX. Pm 275 comments: "Doubt in its sixteen bases, namely, 'Was I not in the past,' etc." (See MN I 8). The three divisions of time are past, future, and present.

62. The three characteristics of impermanence, suffering, and non-self.

63. Pm comments: "'Whatever my materiality, be it in the past, future, or present,' etc." (see Ps, Ñāṇakathā, Section 5).

64. Illumination, knowledge, rapture, tranquillity, bliss, resolve, grasp, indifference, establishing, desire to act. See Vism XX, 105ff.

65. Pm 275 comments: "'Of the nineteen kinds': by way of analysis of the path, fruition, nibbāna, called the overcoming of the defilements to be reviewed. Nineteen because of the absence of residual defilements in the arahat." See Ps, *Ñāṇakathā*, Section 14. The whole paragraph is, in fact, a summary of what is contained in Vism from Chap. XVIII onwards.

66. Pm comments on this paragraph: "'Experienced as object.' What is meant? Just as though, when one going in search of a snake discovers (experiences) its abode, (it is as though) he had already discovered (experienced) it, and caught it, too, owing to the facility with which he (knows he) will catch it by means of charms and medicine. Thus, when the object (which is) become the abode of rapture is experienced (discovered), rapture itself is experienced (discovered), too, owing to the facility with which it is grasped as regards its specific and general characteristics.... 'By his penetration of its characteristics': by penetration of the specific and general characteristics of rapture. When the specific and general characteristics of anything are experienced, then that thing is experienced according to reality." (Pm 276. This passage occurs in Ṭīkā to Paps commenting on this sutta.)

67. "Bliss can be known in two ways: as non-delusion and as object" (Vimm).

68. "He knows in two ways: as non-delusion and as object" (Vimm).

69. Bliss is one of the feelings, but rapture belongs to the formations aggregate.

70. "The mind is aware of entering into, and going out of, the object in two ways—as non-delusion and as object" (Vimm).

71. "'Setting free' means releasing by deliverance consisting of suppressing, separating, abandoning the hindrances. 'At the moment of insight': at the moment of contemplation of dissolution (see Vism XXI, 12). For dissolution is called the culmination of insight. Therefore the meditator who contemplates dissolution by its means sees all that is formed by consciousness as impermanent, not as permanent; and because of the suffering in impermanence and the absence of self in suffering, he sees that also as pain, not as pleasure, as non-self, not as self (Ps I 58). But because what is impermanent, suffering, and non-self is not to be delighted in, and what is not to be delighted in is not to be lusted after therefore, when the formations are seen in accordance with contemplation of dissolution as impermanent, suffering, and non-self, he feels revulsion for them, he does not delight in them, he feels dispassionate towards them, he does not feel passion for them. Feeling revulsion and dispassion, at first by means of mundane knowledge he causes cessation: he does not arouse, does not bring about this arising, is the meaning. Or alternatively, being thus dispassionate, by means of his own knowledge he causes the unseen formations as well as the seen to cease, he does not arouse them; he brings to mind only their cessation, not their arising, is the meaning. Practising thus, he relinquishes, does not cling. What is meant? Because of giving up the defilements together with the kamma-accumulations of the aggregates, and because of entering into Nibbāna, which is their opposite, through inclining thereto owing to seeing the unsatisfactoriness of what is formed; this is called relinquishment as giving up and relinquishment as entering into. Therefore the meditator who is possessed of that gives up the defilements in the way aforesaid and enters into Nibbāna. Hence it was said, 'setting free, releasing the mind from the perception of permanence by means of the contemplation of impermanence at the moment of insight ... setting free, releasing the mind from clinging by means of the contemplation of relinquishment, he breathes in and breathes out'" (Pm 279).

72. "Here, what is this impermanence? Or, how is it impermanence? Or, what is contemplation of impermanence? Or, it is contempla-

tion of impermanence of what? Pointing out that this tetrad should
be explained in this way, he said: 'The impermanent should be
understood,' and so forth. Here, 'permanent' is what is permanent,
eternal—as is Nibbāna. 'Not permanent' is impermanent, possessed
of rise and fall. (Referring to) formed things as to their meaning,
he said: 'Impermanent are the five aggregates. Why? Because of
their rise and fall and change,' meaning that they have the nature
of rise and fall and change. Herein, there having been an arising of
formed things through cause and condition, a state of individual
existence is produced, is 'arisen.' The momentary cessation, anni-
hilation, of these (arisen things) is 'fall.' Alteration through decay
is 'change.' Just as there is no change of basis at the point of arising, nor at the point of breaking up and dissolution, there is likewise no change of basis at the point facing dissolution called presence—in ordinary usage, 'decay.' Therefore, the decay of a single
thing is meant—that which is called momentary decay; and certainly absence of difference of basis in the points of arising and
dissolution is necessary; otherwise one would fall into the fallacy
(of holding) that one thing arises and another is broken up. Therefore it was concerning momentary decay that he said 'change' "
(Pm 279–80).

73. " 'Which occur as seeing both kinds' should be construed as the
occurring of insight in contemplation of fading away as destruction, and the occurring of the path in contemplation of absolute
fading away. Or the occurring of insight in contemplation of fading away as destruction should be understood as object, and in
contemplation of absolute fading away should be understood as
non-delusion in the contemplation of fading away and as object in
the contemplation of absolute fading away" (Pm 280).

74. "Mindfully he breathes in and out (thinking) thus: 'This is transi-
ence, this is dispassion, this is Nibbāna' " (Vimm).

75. "Contemplating the various hindrances according to reality (he
thinks), 'There are the transient things: the destruction of these is
Nibbāna.' Thus with tranquillized vision he trains himself" (Vimm).

76. "Relinquishment which is the giving up of what should be abandoned either by substituting for them their opposite qualities, or by
cutting them off, is 'relinquishment as giving up'; the relinquishment of self in the cessation of forming kamma which is the relin-

quishment of the substrata of existence, or the entering into that either through inclination thereto or through having it as object, is 'relinquishment as entering into.' 'By substituting for them their opposite qualities': herein, firstly, contemplation of impermanence gives up the perception of permanence by abandoning that aspect. Likewise, giving up consists in non-occurrence; all the kamma-formations which are rooted in the defilements owing to the grasping of permanence, and the kamma-resultant aggregates which would arise in the future rooted in both (the kamma-formations and defilements)—these it gives up by causing their non-occurrence. Likewise with the perception of suffering, etc. Hence he said: 'insight gives up the defilements together with the kamma-accumulations of the aggregates by substituting for them their opposite qualities.' 'Through seeing the unsatisfactoriness of what is formed' means through seeing the fault of impermanence in what is formed consisting of the formations of the three planes of existence. 'Opposite' is because of the permanence (of the unformed). 'The path gives up the defilements together with the kamma-accumulation of aggregates': when the defilements are given up by the path, the kamma-accumulations are called 'given up' because they no longer have any means of effecting result, and the aggregates which are rooted therein are called 'given up', because there is no opportunity for their arising. 'Both' are insight knowledge and path knowledge, for path knowledge is called a contemplation because of seeing Nibbāna immediately after change-of-lineage (maturity) knowledge" (Pm 281).

77. "Discerning states of wretchedness according to reality, (he thinks), 'these are transient,' and freeing himself from states of wretchedness, he abides in the peace of Nibbāna. Thus he trains himself and attains to bliss. The tranquil and the sublime are to be understood thus: all activities are brought to rest; all defilements are forsaken; craving is destroyed; passion is absent; it is the peace of blowing out" (Vimm).

78. "All formations are possessed of applied thought and sustained thought. That being so, why is only applied thought suppressed in respiration-mindfulness and not the other? It is used here in a different sense. Discursiveness is a hindrance to jhāna. In this sense it is suppressed" (Vimm).

"Why is air contact pleasant? Because it calms the mind. It is comparable to the soothing of the mind by a minstrel spirit with sweet sounds. By its means applied thinking is suppressed. And again, it is like one walking by the banks of a river. His mind is collected and directed towards one object and does not wander" (Vimm).

79. This is the end of the section of Vism on respiration mindfulness. What follows is from Paps, commenting on MN No. 118.

80. *Kāya* here has its double meaning of "body" and "group." See also Ps II 232, where "earth, water, fire, and air bodies" and others are listed.

81. Pleasant, painful, and neither-pleasant-nor-painful (neutral) feeling.

82. " 'Arrived at tranquillity': he looks with equanimity on the mind which has arrived at the central state of equipoise which is the sign of tranquillity. 'Establishment as one': establishment by way of a single state through the disappearance of opposition" (Ṭīka).

83. "'Not only the mental objects beginning with the hindrances': having seen only the mental objects beginning with the hindrances to be abandoned, then having seen correctly through understanding also the knowledge of abandoning of these, he becomes one who looks on with equanimity. For this is said by the Blessed One (at MN I 135), '(Good) things, bhikkhus, should be abandoned—how much more so bad things'" (Ṭīka).

84. The next three paragraphs are from Paps I 85 (commenting on MN I 11), to which the commentary on MN No.118 refers.

Part III : The Paṭisambhida-magga

1. For convenience "breathing in" is referred to as a "mode," likewise "breathing out." The two taken together are referred to as a "base," of which there are four in each of the four tetrads.

2. "Respiration-mindfulness" (*ānāpānasati = āna + apāna + sati*): "Ānaṃ is the wind entering inwards. *Apānaṃ* is the wind issuing outwards. But some say it is the other way round" (Sdhp 320).

3. "It establishes the unities in the first place in the plane of access, through the absence of distraction by many objects" (Sdhp 321).

4. "Hindrances in the sense of shutting off the way of approach to the outlets" (Sdhp 321).

5. "It is an outlet for the noble ones by way of being the approach to fruition, because the noble path, called the outlet of the noble ones who stand on the path, acts as the cause of that fruition" (Sdhp 321).

6. Reading *khaṇikasamodhānā ime aṭṭhārasa upakkilesā uppajjanti* . "The imperfections that arise do so in connection from moment to moment, in momentary sequence, not in a single moment of consciousness" (Sdhp 321).

7. "Of the breath entering inwards, the nose-tip or the upper lip is the beginning, the heart the middle, and the navel the end. The mind of one who follows with mindfulness the beginning, middle, and end of that in-breath becomes unsteady, and the mind which is unsteady owing to non-establishment of the unities is an obstacle to concentration" (Sdhp 322).

8. "Of the breath issuing outwards, the navel is the beginning, the heart the middle, and the nose-tip or the upper lip or the space outside is the end" (Sdhp 322).

9. "The desire, called the longing for continual gross in-breathing, after concluding that 'this meditation subject is dependent on the passage of wind through the nostrils,' is the occurrence of craving. When craving occurs it is an obstacle to concentration, because there is no establishment of the unities" (Sdhp 322).

10. "The desire, called longing for the out-breathing again preceded by in-breathing" (Sdhp 322).

11. "One who makes a very long or a very short in-breath, and because of the presence of bodily and mental fatigue caused by that in-breath, is irritated and harassed by that in-breath" (Sdhp 322).
    "Greed for the obtaining of the out-breath in one who aspires to out-breath and perceives satisfaction in out-breath just because of being harassed by in-breath" (Sdhp 322).

12. The same explanation applies as in note 11; but change "in-breath" to "out-breath," and conversely.

13. "The 'sign' is the place where the in-breaths and out-breaths touch. For in-breaths and out-breaths as they occur strike the nose-tip of

one with a long nose, and the upper lip of one with a short nose" (Sdhp 323).

14. "Consciousness which follows after in-breath or out-breath which has passed beyond the place of contact and gone away from it" (Sdhp 323).

15. "Consciousness which is expecting and awaiting in-breath or out-breath not yet arrived at the place of contact" (Sdhp 323).

16. "In one bringing to mind the sign of in-breaths and out-breaths, greed arises in regard to the rapture and bliss that have arisen, or in regard to a past subject for laughter, talk, or amusement" (Sdhp 323).

17. "Ill will attacks the mind, either through mental pain which has arisen in the mind that has grown dissatisfied with paying attention to (the meditation subject), or through regarding causes for annoyance formerly experienced" (Sdhp 323).

18. "Consciousness is fixed on the place of contact of the breaths" (Sdhp 324).

19. "Exerting by means of the development of the enlightenment factors of investigation-of-states and rapture" (Sdhp 324).

20. "Restraining by means of the development of the enlightenment factors of tranquillity, concentration, and equanimity. Or 'exerting by means of the faculties of mindfulness and energy, and restraining by means of the faculties of mindfulness and concentration,' they say also" (Sdhp 324).

21. "Clearly comprehending in this case through contemplation of the 'foul' (i.e. the thirty-two parts of the body or the nine charnel ground contemplations), thus he abandons lust" (Sdhp 324).

22. "Clearly comprehending in this second case through contemplation of amity; thus he abandons ill will" (Sdhp 324).

23. "*Dānupasaggupaṭṭhānekatta*: the relinquishment (*upasagga*) of the giving (*dāna*) called the gift (*dānavatthu*) = relinquishment in giving (*dānupasagga*), that is to say, the volition of giving up the gift; the establishing (*upaṭṭhāna*) of that volition, the remaining after approaching it by making it the object of consciousness = establishment of relinquishment in giving (*dānupasaggupaṭṭhāna*); the unity consisting of that, or the unity obtained thereby, is the unity

which is the establishing of relinquishment in giving (*dānupasag-gupatthānekatta*). By deduction, the concentration on the recollection of generosity (see Vism VII, 107) is expressed by this phrase. Also by deduction it is expressed as the decisive-support condition for the other three unities that follow; that is why it is set forth here, they say.

"Or alternatively, as regards these four unities, the first may be understood as expressing access concentration, the second full absorption, the third insight, and the fourth the paths and fruitions" (Sdhp 324).

24. "The 'higher consciousness' is concentration made the basis for insight" (Sdhp 325).

25. "Of those who see by insight the formations by means of the three contemplations beginning with the contemplation of dissolution (see Vism XXI, 10ff. and note 95 below)" (Sdhp 325).

26. "Of the eight noble persons" (Sdhp 325); that is, the path and fruition of stream-entry, once-return, non-return, and arahatship.

27. Reading *patipadāvisuddhipakkhantam*. "The practice itself is the purity because of purification from the stains of the defilements. Entered into, gone into, that purity of practice" (Sdhp 325).

28. "Grown strong, increased, in the equanimity of the central state of equipoise" (Sdhp 325).

29. "Gladdened, cleansed, purified by cleansing knowledge.
"And 'purity of practice' is access with its constituents; 'strengthening in equanimity' is full absorption; 'gladdening' is reflection, according to some. But because 'consciousness become one-pointed is then entered into purity of practice,' and so on, is said, therefore, during full absorption, 'purity of practice' should be understood as the way of arrival, 'strengthening in equanimity' as functioning through the equanimity of the central state of equipoise, and 'gladdening' as the success of the function of cleansing-knowledge by producing a state of non-excess of any mental state. How? At the time when full absorption arises, then the mind is purified from the groups of defilements called hindrances which are an obstacle to that jhāna, and being rid of obstructions because of that purification, it arrives at the central (state which is the) sign of tranquillity" (Sdhp 325).

30. First, second, third, and fourth rūpa (fine-material) jhāna: see MN I 21–22, etc., for description, and Vism, Ch. IV, for full details.

31. Attainment of the sphere of boundless space, of boundless consciousness, of nothingness, and of neither-perception-nor-non-perception; see MN I 41 for description and Vism, Ch. X, for details.

32. Contemplation of impermanence,
    contemplation of suffering,
    contemplation of non-self,
    contemplation of revulsion (*nibbidā*),
    contemplation of fading away (*virāga*),
    contemplation of cessation,
    contemplation of relinquishment,
    contemplation of destruction,
    contemplation of passing away,
    contemplation of change,
    contemplation of the signless,
    contemplation of the desireless,
    contemplation of the void,
    insight into states which is the higher understanding,
    the eye of knowledge according to reality,
    contemplation of danger,
    contemplation of reflection,
    contemplation of turning away (*vivaṭṭa*).

33. The paths of stream-entry, once-return, non-return, and arahatship.

34. " 'The central (state of equipoise which is the) sign of tranquillity' is a name for full absorption which is proceeding evenly. But the consciousness immediately before that, which approaches that state by the method of change in a single continuity, is said to arrive at the central (state of equipoise which is the) sign of tranquillity. Because of having thus arrived, it is said to enter into that full absorption through the approach to that state" (Sdhp 326).

35. "Thus, in the first place (see last note), purity of practice should be understood as providing the cause existing in the consciousness preceding full absorption, in the sense of approach to the actual moment of arising of the first jhāna.

"But, while doing no work of purifying owing to the absence of need for further purification of the mind thus purified, it is said that 'the purified mind looks on with equanimity.' And while doing no work of further concentrating the mind that has arrived at tranquillity through the approach to the state of tranquillity aforesaid, it is said that 'being arrived at tranquillity, it looks on with equanimity.' And lastly, while doing no work of further establishing the unities in the mind that is already established through unity by abandoning its contact with the defilements owing to the very fact of having arrived at tranquillity, it is said that 'having established the unities, it looks on with equanimity' " (Sdhp 326).

36. "At this time the pair of states called concentration and understanding [Note: elsewhere usually referred to as tranquillity and insight (*samatha-vipassanā*)] which came into being when the mind was thus strengthened in equanimity, proceed evenly, without either one exceeding the other; and the faculties of faith, etc., proceed with a single nature through having the nature of deliverance, because of being delivered from the various defilements, and the energy which is in conformity therewith, which is suitable to their non-excess and single nature, has sustaining power; and cultivation occurs in that moment. And all these aspects are produced through knowledge because of gladdening, purifying, and cleansing, accordingly after seeing the various dangers in the defilements and advantages in purification. Therefore, 'gladdening' should be understood as the accomplishment of the function of knowledge which cleanses by consolidating the non-excess and single nature of those states.

"And in this connection, 'gladdening,' as a function of knowledge, is called 'the end' since knowledge due to equanimity is made clear in the passage: 'the mind thus exerted looks on with complete equanimity'; then the understanding faculty is predominant by virtue of understanding due to equanimity. Through equanimity the mind is liberated from variety and defilements; then the understanding faculty is predominant by virtue of understanding due to liberation. Because of being liberated, these states come to be of a single nature; then the understanding faculty is predominant by virtue of understanding due to development in the sense of single nature (Ps II 25)" (Sdhp 326).

37. " 'The sign for the binding' is the nose-tip or the upper lip, which is the cause and the sign for the binding of mindfulness" (Sdhp 328).

38. The last lines = Dhp 382; the whole verse = Thag 548.

39. The Pāli reads: "*ānan' ti assāso no pasāso*," "*apānan' ti passāso no assāso*." Punctuation in PTS text is misleading.
    The object of this passage seems to be that of equating *āna* with *assāsa*, and *apāna* with *passāsa*, in order to make certain which is being referred to.

40. "Perfected by the attainment of the arahat path successively through jhāna, insight, and the (lower) paths. And 'in the sense of laying hold,' and so on, is said with reference to these things, namely, jhāna, insight, and the paths. For these things are 'layings hold' because of being laid hold of by one who meditates; accordingly it is perfected in the sense of laying hold. And because of the converging there in mutual relationship of all the mental faculties it is 'perfected in the sense of converging.' And through the perfecting of development it is 'perfected in the sense of perfecting' " (Sdhp 329).

41. "On whatever one of the sixteen bases of respiration-mindfulness" (Sdhp 330).

42. "At the moment of the arahat path 'self-taming' is the gentleness of the self; 'tranquillizing' is cooling; 'extinction' is extinction of defilement; 'direct knowledge' is by way of all states; 'full understanding' is the function of path knowledge; 'complete comprehension of the truths' is seeing the four truths with a single (simultaneous) penetration; 'establishment of cessation' is making cessation the object of consciousness" (Sdhp 332).

43. Pleasant, painful, and neither-pleasant-nor-painful feeling.

44. "Material food, sense-impression, mental volition, consciousness" (MN I 48).

45 Materiality, feeling, perception, formations, consciousness (see SN XXII, 48).

46. Eye, ear, nose, tongue, body, mind (see SN XXXV, and MN I 52, etc.)

47. (1) Sense-sphere, (2) Brahmā's retinue, (3) Ābhassara deities, (4) Subhakiṇṇa deities, (5) sphere of boundless space, (6) sphere of boundless consciousness, (7) sphere of nothingness. (See DN III 253.)

48. Gain, fame, blame, pleasure, and their opposites. (See DN III 260.)

49. (1) Sense-sphere, (2) Brahmā's retinue, (3) Ābhassara deities, (4) Subhakiṇṇa deities, (5) unconscious beings, (6) sphere of boundless space, (7) sphere of boundless consciousness, (8) sphere of nothingness, (9) sphere of neither-perception-nor-non-perception. (See DN III 263.)

50. Eye, visible-object; ear, sound; nose, odour; tongue, flavour; body, tangible-object. (See SN XXXV and MN I 111–12.)

51. As the last, plus mind and mental object.

52. Eye, visible-object, eye-consciousness;
    ear, sound, ear-consciousness;
    nose, odour, nose-consciousness;
    tongue, flavour, tongue-consciousness;
    body, tangible object, body-consciousness;
    mind, mental object, mind-consciousness.   (See MN III 62.)
    This particular form of list is a device used in several instances in the *Paṭisambhidā Ñāṇakathā* first section, where it appears in various forms. It is also the formula of the *Kumārapañha* of the *Khuddakapāṭha*.

53. The demon who is supposed to take the moon in his mouth during an eclipse.

54. " 'A noble commoner' is a commoner, i.e. one who has not attained (the paths), through his not having cut off the defilements (by attaining the path); he is noble through his devotion to the observance of training; he trains in the higher training. 'A trainer' (*sekha*) is a stream-enterer, a once-returner, or a non-returner. An arahat possesses the state of fruition which is unshakable and incapable of being moved" (Sdhp 349).

55. The exact significance of some of these terms is not clear at this distance of time. Pm 350 comments " 'Dwelling': any of the remaining dwellings mentioned (in the Vinaya) except a 'half-gabled building,' etc. 'Half-gabled building' is like a bird's crooked

wing. 'Palace': a long palace built with two stories. 'Mansion': a gabled palace built on a levelled space. 'Cave': a brick hut, stone hut, wooden hut or mud hut." So it is stated in the commentary to the Khandhakas (see Vin. Cullavagga, 158, and Samantapāsādikā). But in the Vibhaṅga Commentary a 'dwelling' is an abode constructed entirely within a surrounding path, showing it is for use day and night; and a 'cave' is an underground cave where a lamp is needed day and night.

56. " 'In the sense of laying hold': in the sense of being laid hold of. What is laid hold of? The outlet. What outlet? Respiration-mindfulness concentration itself is the outlet, as far as the arahat path. Hence he said, 'In the sense of outlet.' It is by the meaning of the word *mukha* as foremost that the meaning of 'outlet from the round of rebirths' is expressed. 'In the sense of establishing' is just in the sense of its own nature. But the meaning expressed by all these words is: 'having made mindfulness the outlet which is laid hold of.' Some, however, explain as follows: 'in the sense of laying hold' means in the sense of laying hold with mindfulness; 'in the sense of outlet' means in the sense of the door of entry and exit of the in-breaths and out-breaths; then, 'having established mindfulness as the outlet of the in-breaths and out-breaths which is laid hold of,' is what is said" (Sdhp 350–51).

57. " 'Reckoned as a long extent' means in a time called long; for a long road is called 'an extent,' and this time is so called as though it actually were an extent because of its length" (Sdhp 351).

58. "After saying firstly, 'he breathes in' and 'he breathes out,' and 'in-breaths' and 'out-breaths,' separately, they are combined together in the expression, 'he breathes in and breathes out,' in order to show the uninterrupted process of development" (Sdhp 351).

59. " 'Zeal arises': zeal is produced through increased progress in development" (Sdhp 351). Pm, commenting independently on this passage where it is quoted in Vism, says: "Owing to the pleasure obtained by the gradual bringing about of attainment through development, profitable desire arises, here specially characterized by desire to act" (Pm 260).

60. " 'Joy arises': rapture is produced owing to the perfecting of the development" (Sdhp 351). Pm says: "Through the more subtle state

of the in-breaths and out-breaths, through the increased peaceful-
ness of the object, through the advancement of the meditation subject, there arises joy for the mind devoted to development, namely,
rapture of the lesser and other kinds" (Pm 260–61). The five kinds
of rapture are given as lesser rapture, momentary rapture, flooding
rapture, transporting rapture, and ecstatic rapture (PTS Dict., under
pīti).

61.   " 'The mind turns away': when the counterpart sign dependent on
      the in-breaths and out-breaths arises, the mind turns away from the
      original in-breaths and out-breaths" (Sdhp 351). Pm says: "The
      mind turns away from those (breaths) which have reached a point
      approaching non-manifestation owing to their occurring with ever
      more extreme subtlety. But some (say) that when the in-breaths
      and out-breaths have reached a more subtle state, then, when the
      counterpart sign has arisen, the mind turns away from the original
      in-breaths and out-breaths" (Pm 261).

62.   " 'Equanimity is established': the central state of equipoise is es-
      tablished because of the absence, due to the production of access
      or full absorption in that counterpart sign, of (need for) further
      work of concentrating" (Sdhp 351).

63.   " 'The body': the in-breaths and out-breaths as particles constitute
      'the body' in the sense of a mass. And the sign which has arisen in
      dependence on the original in-breath and original out-breath is also
      given the name 'in-breath and out-breath' " (Sdhp 351).

64.   " 'The establishment (foundation) is mindfulness': the mindfulness
      defined as 'having arrived at that object, it remains' is the 'estab-
      lishment' " (Sdhp 351).
      Satipaṭṭhāna (establishment, or foundation, of mindfulness) is
      derived consistently by the *Paṭisambhidā* from *sati* (mindfulness)
      and *upaṭṭhāna* (establishment—but this word also means "appear-
      ance" and "waiting on," among other things). The sutta com-
      mentaries, however, favour derivation from *sati* and *paṭṭhāna*
      ("foundation"—see Paps I 237–38; commentary to MN No.10).
      The paragraph in question is repeated for each of the sixteen bases
      with the purpose of showing which of the four *satipaṭṭhāna* is being
      practised. There is no English word which quite straddles these
      two meanings; hence the clumsy device adopted here of coupling
      the two words "establishment" and "foundation" together.

65. " 'Contemplation is knowledge': as tranquillity it is contemplation of the sign-body, and as insight it is contemplation of the mentality-body that is knowledge, is the meaning" (Sdhp 351). Pm states more fully: " 'Contemplation is knowledge': as tranquillity, it is contemplation of the sign-body (that is knowledge); and as insight, it is contemplation of mentality-materiality by defining the in-breaths and out-breaths and the body on which they depend as 'materiality,' and consciousness and the states associated therewith as 'the immaterial' that is knowledge, which here means understanding according to reality" (Pm 261).

66. " 'The body is the establishment (foundation)': that body is called the establishment, since mindfulness, having approached (it), remains (is stabilized) there. 'But it is not mindfulness': but it is not that body that is called mindfulness, is the meaning" (Sdhp 351).

67. " 'Mindfulness is both the establishment (foundation) and mindfulness' in the sense of remembering and in the sense of establishing" (Pm 261).

68. " 'By means of that mindfulness' and 'by means of that knowledge' here stated, having approached that aforesaid body with tranquillity and insight, he sees by means of knowledge associated with jhāna, or by means of insight knowledge. This sentence contains the word 'body' with reference to the passage (that follows, namely), 'The development of the establishment (foundation) of mindfulness consisting of contemplation of the body in the body' that has now to be stated, because this tetrad is stated by way of contemplation of the body, although the words 'body' and so on, are absent in the list (of bases) itself" (Sdhp 351–52).

69. " 'Contemplation of the body in the body' is contemplation of that body in a manifold body; or alternatively, it is contemplation of the body, not contemplation of any other state, in the body, is what is said. Not the contemplation of permanence, pleasure, self in the body which is impermanent, painful, non-self, but rather contemplation of that very body as impermanent, painful, non-self. Or alternatively, contemplation of just that mere body itself, because of non-contemplation of anything to be taken as 'I' or 'mine' or 'woman' or 'man.' Likewise, below, in the three cases of 'contemplation of the feelings in the feelings,' etc.

"Mindfulness itself as the establishment (foundation) is 'the establishment (foundation) of mindfulness'; the establishment (foundation) of mindfulness which is associated with contemplation of the body is 'the establishment (foundation) of mindfulness consisting of contemplation of the body'; the development of that is 'the development of the establishment (foundation) of mindfulness consisting of contemplation of the body.'

"'That body': although the mentality-materiality body is not expressly stated, it is nevertheless as though it had been, because of its being included in the word 'body'; for the contemplations of impermanence and so on are only applicable to the mentality-materiality body, not to the sign-body. 'Contemplation' and 'development' have the aforesaid meanings" (Sdhp 352).

70. "This section is given in order to point out the benefits of the development of respiration-mindfulness. For its benefits are the enrichment of mindfulness and the enrichment of knowledge. Herein, 'for one who knows one-pointedness and non-distraction of mind' is said with reference to the one-pointednes of mind at the time of insight in one who has obtained jhāna. 'Feelings are known': feelings are known in general by seeing them rise; 'known as they appear': they appear known as destructible, perishable, and void; 'known as they subside': known in general by seeing fall; they subside, break up, is the meaning. The same applies to perception and applied thoughts. But when these three are stated, the remaining immaterial states are also stated. But why are only these three stated? Because of difficulty in grasping. As regards the feeling, among these the pleasant and painful are evident, but the neither-pleasant-nor-painful is subtle, difficult to grasp, and unevident; though it is evident to him. Perception, because it only grasps aspects, does not grasp things according to their true nature; and, when it is associated with insight knowledge, which grasps specific and general characteristics, it is very unevident; though that also is evident to him. Applied thought, because of its resemblance to knowledge, is difficult to lay hold of apart from knowledge, according as it is said, 'That which is right view, friend Visākha, and that which is right thinking—these things are included in the understanding group (of the Eightfold Path)' (MN I 301); though that applied thought also is evident to him" (Sdhp 353).

This section, which is also repeated for all the sixteen bases, would appear to present the practice of mindfulness and clear comprehension, since it coincides with an Aṅguttara Nikāya sutta which runs, "And how, bhikkhus, does concentration being developed and much practised lead to mindfulness and clear comprehension? Here, bhikkhus, for a bhikkhu, feelings are known as they arise, known as they appear, known as they subside; perceptions are known as they arise …; applied thoughts are known as they arise …," etc. (AN II 45; cf. MN III 124). The prime importance of mindfulness and clear comprehension (*sati-sampajañña*) is given full emphasis in MN No.10 and its commentary.

71.   " 'With the arising of ignorance … with the cessation of ignorance,' etc.: in the section on applied thoughts, instead of saying, 'with the arising of sense-impression … with the cessation of sense-impression,' 'with the arising of perception… with the cessation of perception' is said. Why is that? Because applied thought is rooted in perception, for 'variety of thinking arises due to variety of perception' is said" (Sdhp 353).

72.   "As regards 'To one who brings them to mind as impermanent,' and so on, it should be construed in each as: 'To one who brings feeling to mind as impermanent.' But, since the feeling which is associated with insight is of no help to insight because it is incapable of accomplishing the function of insight, it has not been handed down among (what are called) the 'states partaking of enlightenment.' But the function of perception associated with insight is obscure, too, therefore, that too is of no help to insight. But there is no function of insight without applied thought. For insight accomplishes its own function with applied thought as its companion, as it is said (at Vism XVI, 99), 'Understanding is not able, of its own nature, to define an object as impermanent, painful, non-self; but, when applied thought is present repeatedly striking, it can. For just as a money-changer who has a coin in his hand and wishes to look at it on all sides, cannot turn it over with the power of his eye alone, but he can look at it on all sides by turning it over with his finger-tips; so, indeed, understanding is not able, of its own nature, to define an object as impermanent, etc., but it is able, when a thing is given, to define it by means of applied thought, which has the characteristic of focusing, and the nature of beating

and striking, as though hitting and turning over.' That is why, because of the unhelpfulness of feeling and perception to insight,
they are in certain instances set forth in the singular in order to
show them by way of mere characteristic only, whereas applied
thought in certain instances is set forth in the plural in order to
show that there are as many kinds of applied thoughts as of insight" (Sdhp 353).

73.   *Samodhāneti* = "brings together," "combines"; it has here been ren-
dered "brings to bear." In pursuing this meditation as so far described, he is at the same time giving effect to all the things listed
in this paragraph, which is repeated for all sixteen bases.

    "'Combines' means places as object, sets up as object; also in the
absence of any work of bringing together, he brings together, just
by means of the perfection of the development itself. 'The domain' is formations as object at the moment of insight, and Nibbāna
as object at the moment of the path and moment of fruition. 'The
meaning of calm' (*samatha*) is calm (*samaṃ*) itself as the meaning
(*attha*); or it is the meaning of calm (*samass'attho*)" (Sdhp 353).

74.   "The mental objects consisting of the faculties, the powers, and the
enlightenment factors, are obtained at the moments of insight, path,
and fruition; the path and the three purities only at the moments of
path and fruition; liberation and clear vision and knowledge of destruction only at the moment of the path; deliverance and knowledge of non-arising only at the moment of fruition; the rest at the
moment of insight—thus in this section on mental objects he brings
to bear these mental objects in this object, and, excepting Nibbāna,
the rest should be understood according as they apply" (Sdhp 354).

75.   "As regards the exposition of 'short,' 'which takes a brief time'
means in a time called brief. The rest is as aforesaid" (Sdhp 355).

76.   "As regards the exposition of 'experiencing the whole body,' feeling which feels the object as agreeable or disagreeable is stated
first for the purpose of easy grasping, owing to the grossness of
feeling among the immaterial states; next, perception which grasps
aspects in the province of feeling thus, 'what he feels he perceives'
(MN I 293); next, volition which forms by means of perception;
next, sense-impression because of the passage, 'touched he feels,
touched he perceives, touched he wills' (SN IV 68); next attention

which has the characteristic of being shared by all these; thus the formations aggregate is stated by volition and so on. So when three aggregates (i.e. feeling, perception, and formations) have been stated, the consciousness aggregate is also stated (by implication). 'Mentality' is of the kind aforesaid; 'and the mentality body'; this is said, however, in order to exclude Nibbāna. Nibbāna is included by 'mentality,' but since insight into supramundane states has not been attained, the word 'body' excludes Nibbāna, since Nibbāna is not included in a collection. 'And those (things) which are called the mental formations'; the mental formations being stated thus, 'perception and feeling are mental properities; these things, being bound up with the mind, are mental formations' (MN I 301); they are here included in the mentality body, too, is what is said" (Sdhp 355).

77.   " 'Great primaries' are earth, water, fire, and air. 'The materiality derived from the four great primaries' means materiality which occurs derived from, depending on, not apart from, the four great primaries; it is twenty-fourfold, namely, eye-, ear-, nose-, tongue-, and body-sensitivity, visible object, sound, odour, flavour, femininity, masculinity, vitality, physical base of mind, nutrition, bodily intimation, verbal intimation, space, physical agility, elasticity, tractability, growth, continuity, decay, and impermanence. 'In-breath and out-breath' are just the normal (breaths). Also the counterpart sign which has arisen dependent on those in-breaths and out-breaths has the same name, as in the case of the earth device (see Vism IV, 31); and because of its resemblance to materiality it has the name 'materiality' as well as in the case of 'he sees forms externally' (MN II 12), and so on. 'And the sign for the binding (of mindfulness)' is the place of contact of the in-breaths and out-breaths, which has become the sign for the binding of mindfulness. 'And those things which are called the bodily formations': the bodily formations being stated thus, 'in-breaths and out-breaths are bodily properties, these things, being bound up with the body, are the bodily formations' (MN I 301); they are here included in the materiality body, is what is said" (Sdhp 355).

78.   " 'Those bodies are experienced': at the moment of jhānas the sign-body of the in-breaths and out-breaths, at the moment of insight the remaining materiality and immaterial bodies, are experienced

as object; at the moment of the path, they are experienced as non-delusion. Also 'through breathing in long,' etc., is stated with reference to the insight and the path that have arisen in one who has obtained jhāna by means of in-breathing and out-breathing" (Sdhp 355–56).

79.   " 'Purity of conduct in the sense of restraint' is just the restraint in jhāna, insight, and the path, which have arisen due to in-breathings and out-breathings stated as 'experiencing the whole body.' 'Purity of consciousness in the sense of non-distraction' is just non-distraction. 'Purity of view in the sense of seeing' is just understanding. 'Restraint' is simply the absence of evil in abstaining from it, and absence thereof during jhāna and insight" (Sdhp356).

80.   "As regards the exposition of 'calming,' and so on, 'bodily properties' means states in the material body; 'bound up with the body' means dependent on the body, when the body is there they come to be, when it is not, they do not. Therefore, as they are formed only by the body, they are bodily formations. 'Calming' means causing to be extinguished, to subside; by the word 'calming,' gross calming is implied. 'Causing to cease' means causing to cease through the non-arising of the gross formations. 'Pacifying' means inducing a peaceful state in the gross formations by means of change in a single continuity" (Sdhp 356).

81.   I.e. the wind of the breaths in the nostrils.

82.   " 'The sign' is an aspect of these sounds; and the sign of the sound is no other than the sound" (Sdhp 358).

83.   Cf. Dhs §9. "The rest of this base should be understood in the way already explained" (Sdhp 358).

84.   " 'Two kinds of bliss' is said for the purpose of showing the two planes, tranquillity and insight; for mental bliss belongs to the plane of tranquillity and the plane of insight. 'Bodily' means of the sensitivity body; it is linked to that because it does not arise without it" (Sdhp 358).

85.   Cf. Dhs §10.

86.   Cf. Dhs §6.

87.   The same formula as that for defining rapture is used to define gladdening.

88. Cf. Dhs § 11.

89. " 'In the sense of rise and fall': 'the state of rise and fall' is the meaning. And here 'five aggregates' is the characteristic of their nature, 'rise and fall' is the characteristic of alternation; 'through absence after having become they are impermanent' is what is stated by that. Hence, too, in the Commentary, after stating their rise and fall and change thus, 'impermanence comes to be through the characteristic of being formed,' also 'absence after having become' is said: 'the quality of absence after having become is the characteristic of impermanence' is what is stated by that" (Sdhp 361).

90. See Ps 55 (*Ñāṇakathā*): "He sees the arising of the materiality aggregate in the sense of conditioned arising thus: (1) with the arising of ignorance there is the arising of materiality; (2) with the arising of craving ...; (3) ... kamma ...; (4) ... nutriment there is the arising of materiality; and (5) one who sees the characteristic of birth sees the arising of materiality." Thus these five characteristics apply in respect of each of the five aggregates, but in the cases of feeling, perception, and formations, substituting "sense-impression" for "nutriment," and in the case of consciousness, substituting "mentality-materiality" for "nutriment."
  In the case of fall, "he sees the fall of the materiality aggregate in the sense of conditioned cessation thus: (1) with the cessation of ignorance there is the cessation of materiality; (2) with the cessation of craving ...; (3) ... kamma ...; (4) ... nutriment there is the cessation of materiality; and (5) one who sees the characteristic of change sees the fall of materiality." These also make twenty-five with the five aggregates (making the same substitutions). Both together make up the fifty. See also Section 14 on p.68.

91. These 201 states from "materiality" to "old-age-and-death" form the basic list of all states to be directly known, etc., in the first section of the *Paṭisambhidā Ñāṇakathā*. The list is frequently referred to later in the *Paṭisambhidā*, usually elided as "*rūpa ... jarā-maraṇaṃ.*" It forms a classified comprehensive list of phenomena in the round of rebirths. See also Vism XX, 6–12.

92. "Seeing danger in the materiality aggregate in the aforesaid sense of impermanence, etc., since starting the contemplation of dissolution; 'fading away of materiality' is Nibbāna, for, on arriving at

Nibbāna, materiality fades away, ceases, by becoming not subject to further arising. 'He is resolute in faith': he is certain about that Nibbāna. 'His mind is firmly decided' means his mind is thoroughly decided, thoroughly fixed by way of object on the dissolution of materiality called destruction and fading away, and by way of hearsay (i.e. what he has not yet himself realized) on Nibbāna as the fading away of materiality called absolute fading away" (Sdhp 361).

93. "The same applies to the contemplation of cessation but with the difference of the paragraph beginning 'Seeing danger through ignorance in these ways.' Herein, by showing the cessation of the dangers of the links of the dependent origination beginning with ignorance, the cessation of the dangers of materiality, etc., are shown also, because the latter do not exceed the limits of the former. And by this special clause the superiority of contemplation of cessation over contemplation of fading away is stated" (Sdhp 361).

94. As regards the exposition of the phrase, 'contemplating relinquishment,' 'gives up materiality' means that through seeing danger he gives up the materiality aggregate by disregarding it. By relinquishment as 'giving up,' relinquishment in the sense of giving up, is what is said. The meaning of 'giving up' is expressed by this word, 'relinquishment.' Therefore, the meaning is: abandoning of the defilements. And here 'insight leading to emergence' gives up the defilements by substituting for them their opposite qualities, and the path does so by cutting them off. 'The entering of the mind into the cessation of materiality, into Nibbāna, means that 'insight leading to emergence' enters into it owing to inclination towards it, and the path does so by making it its object. By 'relinquishment as entering into': relinquishment in the sense of entering into, is what is said. The meaning of 'entering into' is expressed by this word, 'relinquishment.' Therefore the meaning is: the departure of the mind in Nibbāna" (Sdhp 362).

95. In order to understand Sections V to X, it is necessary to refer to the first twelve sections of the *Paṭisambhidā Ñāṇakathā*, chapter on knowledge, and to Vism, Chap. XXI. The *Ñāṇakathā* in its first sections analyses in successive stages of knowledge the progress from the first hearing about the Teaching to the attainment of path and fruition. These stages are:

(1) Knowledge of what is heard. One hears and learns about the Teaching.

(2) Knowledge of virtuous conduct. One begins to practise by cultivating virtue.

(3) Knowledge of concentration. Jhāna is attained.

(4) Knowledge regarding relation of states. The beginning of insight: all phenomena are seen to arise and cease due to the arising and cessation of conditions in accordance with dependent origination.

(5) Knowledge of mastery (of groups). All phenomena, grouped as past, future, and present, are seen as impermanent, painful, and non-self, and as arising and ceasing due to conditions.

(6) Knowledge of rise and fall (*udayabbaya-ñāṇa*). One contemplates the arising and passing away of all phenomena, in particular the five aggregates.

(7) Knowledge of insight (*vipassanā-ñāṇa*). After contemplating phenomena as impermanent, etc., one now contemplates, in particular, the dissolution of the consciousness that has them as object. Consequently one feels revulsion for them.

(8) Knowledge of danger (*ādīnava-ñāṇa*). Seeing their dissolution, one contemplates the arising of all formed things as fearful and dangerous, and their non-arising as safety and peace.

(9) Knowledge of indifference to formations (*saṅkhārupekkhā-ñāṇa*). Seeing all formations as fearful produces desire for deliverance from them, which impels one to review them fully in the light of the knowledge so far acquired. Owing to this, one achieves composure at the prospect of abandoning them.

(10) Change-of-lineage (maturity) knowledge (*gotrabhū-ñāṇa*). In achieving composure, one has reached the point from which there is no retreat; and immediately upon that follows change-of-lineage knowledge, which abandons and emerges from the formations externally, and whereby the first partial glimpse of Nibbāna is obtained.

(11) Path knowledge (*magga-ñāṇa*). This follows immediately next, and consciousness makes Nibbāna its object. Path knowledge abandons and emerges from the formations both exter-

nally and internally. Right view and the other seven path factors emerge from wrong view, etc. This is immediately followed by fruition.

(12) Fruition knowledge (*phala-ñāna*). The effort of emergence is now ceased.

The *Visuddhimagga*, Chap. XXI, expands the series of insight
knowledges (6)–(9) into the "eight knowledges and knowledge in
conformity with the path." (6) and (7) = (i) and (ii), respectively;
(8) is expanded into (iii) knowledge of arising of fear (*bhayat'-
upaṭṭhāna-ñāna*), (iv) knowledge of contemplation of danger
(*ādīnavānupassanā-ñāna*), and (v) knowledge of contemplation of
revulsion (*nibbidānupassanā-ñāna*); (9) is expanded into (vi) knowledge of desire for deliverance (*muccitukamyatā-ñāna*), (vii) knowledge of contemplation of reflection (*paṭisaṅkhānupassanā-ñāna*),
(viii) knowledge of indifference to formations, and (ix) conformity
knowledge (*anuloma-ñāna*). Nos. (viii), (ix) (Vism), and (10)
change-of-lineage are together known as "insight leading to emergence" (*vuṭṭhānagāminivipassanā*).

Now, Section V, "Twenty-four Kinds of Knowledge through Concentration" corresponds to (3) above; Section VI, "Seventy-two
Kinds of Knowledge through Insight" to (4); VII, "Eight Kinds of
Knowledge of Revulsion" (*nibbidā-ñāna*) corresponds to (5), (6),
and (7); VIII, "Eight Kinds of Knowledge in Conformity with Revulsion" (*nibbidānuloma-ñāna*) corresponds to (8); IX, "Eight Kinds
of Knowledge of Tranquillization of Revulsion" (*nibbidāpaṭipas–
saddhi-ñāna*) corresponds to (9), (10), and (11); X, "Twenty-one
Kinds of Knowledge of the Bliss of Deliverance" (*vimuttisukha-
ñāna*) corresponds to twelve.

It is the same chain of stages of insight knowledge, slightly differently grouped, which forms the substance of the fourth tetrad.

96.   " 'He knows according to reality' the formations by means of insight knowledge from mastery of groups up to contemplation of
dissolution (i.e. Nos. (5) to (7) in note 95), and he 'sees' with that
same vision of knowledge as though it were seen with the physical
eye. Therefore it is called 'knowledge of revulsion'; it is called
knowledge of revulsion regarding formations, is what is said. Because the knowledge of arising of fear, etc., and of desire for de-

liverance, etc., have been handed down separately below, here only the kinds of insight knowledge as aforesaid should be understood as knowledge of revulsion" (Sdhp 363).

97. "By the phrase, 'The understanding of the appearance of fear,' the three kinds of knowledge, namely, arising of fear, contemplation of danger, and contemplation of revulsion (see Nos. (iii) to (v) under (8) in note 5) are stated. Because these three have the same characteristic, they are called knowledge in conformity with revulsion, owing to their analogy with the knowledge of revulsion last mentioned" (Sdhp 363).

98. "By the phrase, 'The understanding which is reflection and composure' are stated knowledge of desire for deliverance, of contemplation of reflection, and of indifference to formations ((vi) to (viii) under (9) in note 95). Because these three have the same characteristic, conformity knowledge and path knowledge are included by the term 'reflection and composure' as well. And it is because knowledge of indifference to formations and conformity knowledge have reached the acme of revulsion that they are called 'knowledge of tranquillization of revulsion,' owing to the abandoning of the work of producing revulsion. But it is perfectly correct that path knowledge is called knowledge of tranquillization of revulsion, because it arises in one who tranquillizes revulsion. So, omitting knowledge of desire for deliverance, which comes first, as though it belonged to the preceding knowledge in conformity with revulsion, etc., and taking the two last kinds of knowledge, 'reflection and composure' is said in order to include the path. For when desire for deliverance is stated, conformity knowledge is included but not path knowledge, since the latter is not called 'desire for deliverance'; but it is called 'composure,' owing to composure in the accomplishment of its function. And in the commentary also the words 'attainment' and 'fixing' are used, and by taking this path knowledge as 'fixing' in Nibbāna it is called 'composure.' And it is by the word 'composure,' that path knowledge is also included. And knowledge in conformity with revulsion, as regards meaning, is also knowledge of revulsion. So, by its inclusion in knowledge of revulsion, its inclusion, too, is effected by the phrase 'tranquillization of revulsion,' without its inclusion as knowledge in conformity with revulsion (separately)" (Sdhp 364).

99. " 'Knowledge of the bliss of deliverance' means knowledge asso-
     ciated with the bliss of deliverance due to fruition, and knowledge
     of reviewing as object the bliss of deliverance due to fruition" (Sdhp
     364).

Of related interest from BPS

The Path of Purification
Visuddhimagga

Translated by Bhikkhu Ñāṇamoli

The *Visuddhimagga* is the "great treatise" of Theravāda Buddhism, an encyclopedic manual of Buddhist doctrine and meditation written in the fifth century by the great Buddhist commentator, Bhadantacariya Buddhaghosa. The author's intention in composing this book is to organize the various teachings of the Buddha, found throughout the Pāli Canon, into a clear and comprehensive path leading to the final Buddhist goal, Nibbāna, the state of complete purification. In the course of his treatise Buddhaghosa gives full and detailed instructions on the forty subjects of meditation aimed at concentration; an elaborate account of the Buddhist Abhidhamma philosophy; and detailed descriptions of the stages of insight culminating in final liberation. The present transltion by Bhikkhu Ñāṇamoli ranks as an outstanding cultural achievement.

Of related interest from BPS

The Path of Freedom
Vimuttimagga

Translated from the Chinese by Rev. N.R.M. Ehara, Some Thera, & Kheminda Thera

The *Vimuttimagga* is a manual of meditation, evidently based on the experience of Buddhist monks in ancient times and compiled for the guidance of those intent on a contemplative life. The work is composed in accordance with the classical Buddhist division of the path into the three stages of virtue, concentration, and wisdom, culminating in the goal of liberation. It is widely believed that the *Vimuttimagga* may have been the model used by Acariya Buddhaghosa to compose his magnum opus, the *Visuddhimagga*, several centuries later. The older work is marked by a leaner style and a more lively sense of urgency stemming from its primarily practical orientation. The *Vimuttimagga* is generally ascribed to the Arahant Upatissa, a famous Buddhist monk of Sri Lanka who lived in the first century C.E. The original Pāli text of the work no longer exists, but fortunately a Chinese translation of it, made in the sixth century, has survived. It is from that work that the present translation into English has been made.

THE BUDDHIST PUBLICATION SOCIETY

The BPS is an approved charity dedicated to making known the Teaching of the Buddha, which has a vital message for people of all creeds. Founded in 1958, the BPS has published a wide variety of books and booklets covering a great range of topics. Its publications include accurate annotated translations of the Buddha's discourses, standard reference works, as well as original contemporary expositions of Buddhist thought and practice. These works present Buddhism as it truly is—a dynamic force which has influenced receptive minds for the past 2500 years and is still as relevant today as it was when it first arose. A full list of our publications will be sent upon request. Write to:

The Hony. Secretary
BUDDHIST PUBLICATION SOCIETY
P.O. Box 61
54, Sangharaja Mawatha
Kandy • Sri Lanka
E–mail: bps@mail.lanka.net
Website: http: //www.lanka.com/dhamma